BRITAIN IN THE MODERN WORLD

BOOK TWO 1918–1976

J K HARDMAN

COLLINS

Acknowledgements

The author and publishers are grateful to the
following for permission to reproduce the
photographs used in this book:
American History Picture Library Figs. 58, 67
Keystone Press Agency Figs. 13, 14, 23, 24,
34, 36, 39, 40, 42, 46, 51, 55, 57, 60, 62, 65,
70, 78
Novosti Press Agency Figs. 49, 56, 72
Popperfoto Figs. 19, 21, 26, 31, 33, 38, 45,
52, 59, 66, 68, 69, 75, 76, 77
Punch Publications Ltd Figs. 6, 29
Radio Times Hulton Picture Library
Figs. 2, 7, 8, 9, 10, 11, 12, 15, 17, 18, 20, 22,
25, 27, 28, 32, 35, 37, 71, 73

Cover. An Esso Photograph

ISBN 0 00 327219 2
© J.K. Hardman 1978
Printed in Great Britain
Collins Clear-Type Press

CONTENTS

THE VERSAILLES SETTLEMENT, 1919

A Background

1 Fighting in the First World War had stopped on 11 November 1918, after the Germans had signed an armistice (cease-fire). A full peace treaty was to be drawn up later:

 a for this purpose, statesmen of many nations met at Versailles, outside Paris, in 1919.

 b actually, there were several treaties. The most important was that of Versailles, which contained the settlement between the Allies and Germany, signed in the Hall of Mirrors at Versailles on 28 June 1919. Other treaties were signed at Saint-Germain with Austria, at Trianon with Hungary, at Neuilly with Bulgaria and at Sèvres with Turkey.

 c usually the expression 'Versailles Settlement' is taken to mean all these treaties.

Fig. 1   Europe after the Versailles Settlement, 1919.

2 Much of Europe was in turmoil at the time:

 a revolutions had broken out in Russia (where a civil war was still being waged), in Germany and in Austria-Hungary.

 b though the actual material damage in western Europe was limited to northern France and Belgium, there was widespread famine in Germany and Russia; millions of soldiers on both sides had been killed, and a deadly influenza epidemic had killed millions more people.

 c nations who had been subject to foreign rule for centuries, such as the Poles and Czechs, were now demanding the right to freedom and self-government.

3 Aims of the victors at the peace conference:

 a Lloyd George, representing Britain, had no wish to see Germany crushed. The German Navy had been surrendered to Britain (and was soon to scuttle itself at Scapa Flow). Therefore he believed that Germany could no longer menace Britain. Also, before 1914, she had been one of Britain's best customers, so Lloyd George wanted to see her recover economically from the war.

At the same time, he could see that a Germany bearing a grudge about the peace treaty might cause a future war.

He was under great pressure from public opinion in Britain, where people had been led to believe that after the war Germany would be punished, and made to pay for all the damage and losses the Allies had suffered. Thus many people in Britain believed that she would become a land of plenty at Germany's expense, and a tough peace treaty would be imposed.

 b France was represented by Georges Clemenceau ('The Tiger'), who simply wanted to see Germany crushed once and for all, so that she could never again menace France. For instance, he wanted to take all German lands west of the Rhine, which would then form the new French frontier, and strip her of much of her industry and coal.

 c President Woodrow Wilson represented the United States. He believed that war could be prevented in future if all countries followed the 'Fourteen Points' he had drawn up during

the war. Among these were:
Open diplomacy (i.e. no secret treaties).
Free trade, or at least low tariffs between countries.
Disarmament.
Freedom of the seas in peace and war.
Boundaries in Europe to be fixed according to the principle of 'national self-determination' i.e. according to the wishes of their peoples.
A League of Nations to be formed to settle disputes among countries in future.
Wilson was a man of high ideals, but not very practical, e.g. he overlooked the fact that states set up according to nationalities such as Latvia, Lithuania and Estonia might be small and weak, and thus could fall easy prey to a bigger neighbour, such as Germany or Russia.

d Italy, represented by Signor Orlando, came to the conference in high hopes of receiving a large slice of the Austro-Hungarian Empire, as Italy had been promised by the Treaty of London in 1915 by the Allies (her price for entering the war on their side). She was to be disappointed.

e Japan, our ally in the Far East, having secured various former German islands in the Pacific, left the conference early.

B Terms of the Treaties

1 Germany. Lloyd George and Wilson managed to persuade Clemenceau to agree to a compromise, which, however, the Germans considered very harsh:

a Germany, by the 'war guilt' clause of the treaty, was declared responsible for starting the war. This meant that she was ordered to pay the cost of the war to the Allies by means of 'reparations'. The amount proved difficult to fix, and had to be left to a 'Reparations Commission' which arrived at a figure of £6,600,000,000 in 1921, a colossal amount in those days. Germany was to pay by instalments, both of cash and goods, (e.g. ships, coal, and food).

b Germany had to return Alsace-Lorraine to France, and cede the small territory of

Fig. 2   Leaders of the victorious Allies at Versailles (l. to r. Clemenceau, Wilson and Lloyd George).

Fig. 3   Germany after the Treaty of Versailles, 1919.

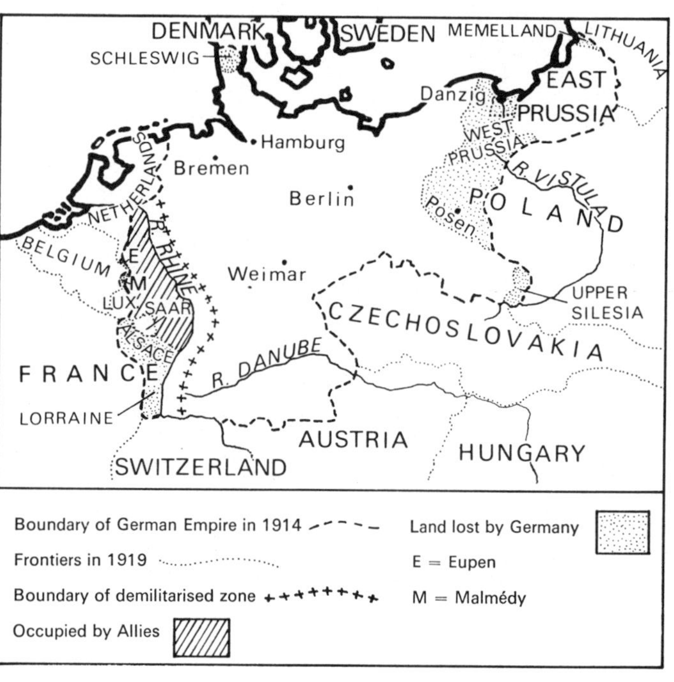

Eupen-Malmédy to Belgium. She lost Schleswig to Denmark, and part of Upper Silesia to Poland after plebiscites. Most of the provinces of Posen and West Prussia went to the new state of Poland. This was done to allow Poland an outlet to the sea, and the majority of the people in Posen were in fact Poles, but the loss cut East Prussia off from the rest of Germany.

As it had a mainly German population, the port of Danzig was declared a 'Free City' under the League of Nations.

Fig. 4 Africa after the Treaty of Versailles, 1919.

The Saar, rich in coal, was to be under international control for fifteen years, during which France would control its coal mines. At the end of that time a plebiscite would be held to allow the people to decide whether to join France or Germany.

c Germany lost all her colonies, which were given to the victors as 'mandates' under the League of Nations.

d Germany's armed forces were severely cut: The army was to be limited to 100 000 men, with no heavy guns or tanks. The General Staff was to be abolished.

The navy was to have no submarines, and no surface ships of more than 10 000 tons each. Germany was to have no air force.

e in Germany itself, the Rhineland and certain crossings over the Rhine were to be demilitarised, i.e. Germany must not fortify them or keep troops there. Also, the Allies would garrison these areas for fifteen years.

f these terms were bitterly resented in Germany, as was the fact that the treaty was a 'Diktat', that is, Germany was allowed no say in drawing it up. Her representatives attended merely to sign what was put before them. Most Germans considered the war guilt clause and reparations grossly unfair. Germany lost one-eighth of her people and some of her coal and heavy industry.

g in fact, Germany never paid anything like the amount of reparations fixed in 1921. Many of the people she lost were not Germans, and she was probably stronger without them. Also, her rapid recovery and later rearmament under Hitler would suggest that her industry was far from crippled by the treaty.

2 Austria. By the Treaty of Saint-Germain Austria lost most of her Empire and became a tiny country of 6 000 000 people:

a she lost the Trentino, Trieste, South Tyrol, and Istria to Italy; and the Dalmatian coast, Bosnia and Herzegovina to the new state of Yugoslavia. Italy was bitterly disappointed at this, (as she had been promised e.g. Dalmatia by the Allies), and left the conference. Austria also lost Galicia to Poland, and Bohemia and Moravia to Czechoslovakia.

b Austria was forbidden ever to join Germany.

3 Hungary, by the Treaty of Trianon, lost Croatia to Yugoslavia, Eastern Slovakia to Czechoslovakia, and Transylvania to Rumania (which also gained Bessarabia from Russia).

4 By the Treaty of Neuilly Bulgaria lost western Thrace to Greece, and some small areas to Yugoslavia.

5 Turkey lost her Empire by the Treaty of Sèvres, which was, however, soon altered.

6 Thus several new states emerged, such as Yugoslavia, Czechoslovakia, Poland (which had been mostly under Russian rule), Lithuania, Latvia and Estonia on the Baltic coast (these three had also been part of Russia), while Finland was declared completely independent of Russia.

7 Under the Treaty of Versailles a League of Nations was set up:

    a there was to be a League Council with five permanent members (the great Powers) and four temporary representatives of smaller nations. The League's assembly was to represent all member nations.

    b the League had its headquarters at Geneva in Switzerland, and its first secretary was an Englishman, Sir John Drummond.

    c member nations agreed, under the League Covenant which they signed on joining, not to resort to force without submitting disputes to League arbitration, to limit armaments, and to support the League by means of economic sanctions against aggressors (i.e. withholding supplies of food or raw materials).

    d on his return to the USA, however, President Wilson found that his own country was not willing to ratify the treaty, or join the League.

8 The Versailles Settlement came under heavy criticism, and had obvious faults, yet given the tremendous problems that they faced, in the circumstances of the time, one must feel some sympathy for the statesmen who drew it up.

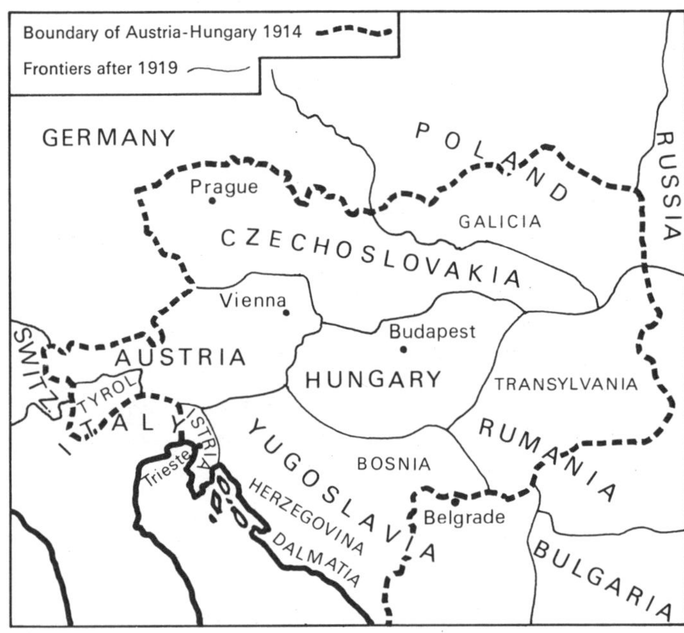

Fig. 5 Dismemberment of the Austro-Hungarian Empire by the Treaties of Saint-Germain and Neuilly, 1919.

Fig. 6 The ghosts of von Moltke, William I and Bismarck look down on Germany's humiliation at Versailles.

BRITAIN, 1918~39

A Position in 1918

Britain seemed to be in a strong position in 1918:

1 She had emerged victorious from a terrible four-year struggle. Under Lloyd George's leadership she had raised a vast army, navy and air force.

2 Despite heavy losses among her troops in France, morale in Britain had remained strong, and now she looked forward to reaping her reward among the victors at the peace conference, and to recovering her old position as the world's largest trading nation.

3 Yet she was to be disappointed. For a year or two after the First World War, Britain enjoyed great prosperity, then a slump set in and by 1921 over two million were out of work. In the years up to 1939 British governments faced serious long-term domestic problems to which they could find no answer.

B Domestic Problems between the Wars

1 Unemployment was the main problem. From 1921 to 1939 the number out of work never dropped below one million and reached a peak of three million in 1933. The main remedy that successive governments tried was to pay the unemployed a dole, as unemployment benefit was called, barely enough to live on. There was no effective government attempt to get at the root of the problem, i.e. to provide work for the unemployed. (A few measures were taken in the 1930s but with little effect.)

2 Effects of the war:

a Britain lost three-quarters of a million men in the war. Yet these numbers were soon made up by the rise in population, and in any case there were too few jobs for the men available.

b Britain's industries had been worked flat-out during the war and much essential maintenance neglected, as in the coal-mines and on the railways. Thus, these industries were in bad shape.

c there was a serious housing shortage, as little house building had been done during the war.

d Britain had lost many of her foreign markets, e.g. for cotton cloth, for ever. Also, she had to sell many of her investments abroad. Before the war the interest on these had helped to pay for much of the food Britain imported. Similarly, her share of the world's shipping had fallen. Thus her 'invisible' earnings dropped.

3 Trading problems. In general, world trade was slow to recover after 1918. The slowness of recovery meant that many countries, such as the USA, put up tariffs to protect their own industries from imports. This made it more difficult for Britain to export to them.

The years between the two World Wars were years of falling prices ('deflation') all over the world, including Britain. This meant that she could import food and raw materials cheaply, but also that the countries who sold her these

Fig. 7 Hunger marchers in the 1930s, making their ineffective protest. Such men had often given up all hope of finding work, and were resigned to life on the 'dole' (unemployment pay). Their housing was often bad, with squalid slum conditions. Food was meagre, often only bread and margarine. Even those who found work were haunted by fear of the 'sack'. For a time the 'means test' was in force. This meant that an unemployed man's total 'means' were taken into account before he became eligible for the dole. This was most humiliating, as it meant that a man could be told to sell some of his furniture, or his children's earnings would be taken into account. This could split families, as a son might resent having to support his father, who in turn would lose his self-respect.

things received less for them. They could not afford to buy much from Britain in return. On the other hand, people with a steady job in Britain benefited from a rising standard of living as prices fell.

4 Problems of particular industries:

a production and exports of cotton had been cut during the war. This meant that many of Britain's former customers, such as India, had to buy elsewhere, or build their own cotton mills. Britain never recovered these markets. Cotton faced a new rival in a man-made fibre, rayon or artificial silk. Also, many of Britain's mills were out-of-date.

b the general fall in trade and a slump in shipbuilding hit the steel industry.

c in coal mining, business was good for a couple of years after the war. Then difficulties arose. Exports fell as ships switched from coal to oil fuel, and other countries' mines, such as those in France, recovered from war damage. Britain's pits were less efficient than many of her rivals' e.g. Germany's. The best seams had been worked out and little mining machinery had been introduced. Also, relations between miners and mine owners were bad. There were serious strikes.

d in shipbuilding, there was a frantic boom until 1920 to make up for losses during the war. This was followed by a serious slump in shipbuilding, as the general fall in world trade meant that fewer ships were needed.

5 Agriculture. A fall in world cereal prices in 1920 meant that the policy of guaranteed prices for farmers (started during the war to encourage food production) was costing the government too much in subsidies, so the Corn Production Act was repealed. This meant that the farmer lost his guaranteed price, and the farm worker lost his guaranteed minimum wage.

6 Financial problems. The war had cost huge sums of money, and the government had had to borrow heavily. Thus the national debt (money borrowed by the government) was very big, and about half the money raised in post-war budgets went to pay interest on it. Also, Britain had borrowed large sums abroad, especially from the USA. Even more was loaned to Britain's Allies, much of which she would never get back (e.g. from Russia).

C The Coalition Government of 1918–22

Domestic policy. Since 1916, David Lloyd George, a Liberal, had led a Coalition Government with Conservative, Liberal, and Labour members. H. H. Asquith, whom Lloyd George had replaced as Prime Minister, led a section of the Liberal Party in opposition. Thus the Liberal Party were split, and were never to recover.

1 The general election ('Coupon Election') of December 1918:

a as soon as the war ended, Lloyd George decided on a general election. Some said he hoped to cash in quickly on his popularity as a victorious war leader. However, there had not been a general election since 1910, the vote had just been given to women over 30 and to many more men (thus trebling the electorate, or number of people entitled to vote), and he was right to seek a vote of support before going to represent Britain at Versailles.

Fig. 8   A comfortably-off family in the 1930s. For people with a secure job, the years between the two World Wars brought a steady increase in the standard of living.

b the Labour Party left the Coalition, and decided to fight the election as an independent party. The Liberals were still split. Some supported Lloyd George and the Coalition, others still supported Asquith, who refused to serve under Lloyd George and thus made reunion impossible. To make clear to the voters which candidates supported the Coalition, Lloyd George and Bonar Law, the Unionist leader, sent out letters to candidates who supported it. Asquith called these letters 'coupons'.

c (the name 'Unionist' was used until 1922, when the partition of Ireland came into force, by the Conservatives and their allies the Liberal Unionists. The latter were a section of the Liberal Party who had split from the main body of the Party in the 1880s over the issue of home rule for Ireland, which Conservatives and Liberal Unionists had opposed.)

d in home affairs, Lloyd George promised jobs for all, plenty of housing ('homes fit for heroes'), and home rule for southern Ireland.

e as far as the peace was concerned, Lloyd George favoured a moderate peace with Germany, but his supporters promised the voters a comfortable future by 'making the Huns pay' and 'squeezing Germany until the pips squeak', as well as hanging the Kaiser.

f the Coalition scored a massive victory, gaining 478 seats. Only 28 Asquith Liberals were elected. Labour, for the first time, became the largest opposition party in the Commons, with 63 seats. (Ireland returned 73 Sinn Fein members, including the first woman, but they did not take their seats.)

2 The most pressing problem was to demobilise the armed forces, i.e. return most of the fighting services to civilian life. This was handled badly. Troops abroad and at home, annoyed by delay, went on strike, and so the government had to bring in a simple system of 'first in first out', i.e. men with the longest service were demobilised first. Thus millions returned to civilian life, where most of them found jobs easily, for a while at any rate.

3 Economic policy:

a during the war, especially after Lloyd George became Prime Minister, the policy of 'war socialism' or state control of the economy, had been greatly extended. Wages, prices and profit levels had all been fixed by the government, and some industries, e.g. the railways and coal mines, had been taken over by the state. Now, in a bid to return to the 'good old days' of laissez-faire (i.e. free enterprise with as little state intervention as possible), these controls were scrapped.

b the result was rapid inflation, with rising prices. The trade union movement was in a strong position, with full employment and eight million members. There were widespread strikes for higher wages, among dockers, factory and railway workers, and even the police. These strikes were usually successful during the post-war boom.

c the 'triple alliance' of miners, railwaymen and transport workers was re-established in 1919, and Lloyd George prevented a miners' strike by appointing a Commission under Sir John Sankey to consider the problems of the coal industry. The Commission recommended better wages and shorter hours for the miners, and a government re-organisation of the industry, i.e. some form of public management. Lloyd George granted the first two points but not the third.

d a miners' strike was thus put off for a time, but in 1921 the mines were handed back to the control of their hundreds of private owners. By now there was a slump and the mine owners demanded cuts in wages and 'district agreements' i.e. that wages and hours should be fixed locally, not nationally as the miners wanted.

e the miners found themselves locked out in April 1921, and on the 15th, 'Black Friday', their supporters in the triple alliance refused to come out on strike in support, so that the miners were forced to go back to work on the owners' terms. The miners' defeat and the rise in unemployment led to reductions of wages for other workers.

4 The National Insurance Act, 1920. This helped to lessen the hardships of being out of work by extending unemployment and sickness benefits to most workers, and extending the time for which benefit could be paid. Yet even so, many were forced to apply for Poor Law relief, which was still a matter for local councils, being paid for out of the rates. This meant that the Boards of Guardians who ran the Poor Law locally, often had trouble, in areas of high unemployment, in raising enough money to pay benefit. In Poplar (London), a number of local councillors were sent to prison for refusing to reduce the levels of Poor Law benefits.

5 The 'Geddes Axe'. As the slump grew worse in 1922, the government's revenue fell, and a cry went up for cuts in government spending. Therefore Lloyd George appointed Sir Eric Geddes to head a special committee to find ways of doing this. The result was the 'Geddes Axe'. Government spending was cut e.g. on the armed forces, but education suffered most. Teachers' salaries were cut, as were school building and nursery classes.

6 Housing. Dr. Addison, Minister of Health, was responsible for a Housing Act in 1919. This required local councils to find out and tell the government what houses were needed, and the government offered a subsidy for each house a local council built to rent. Unfortunately, the act came into force when building costs were high, so the houses proved dear to build.

These subsidies were abolished by the 'Geddes Axe', and Addison was sacked by Lloyd George. Still, the act meant that for the first time the government had taken direct action to help the building of houses.

7 Ireland's position in 1918:

a in theory the whole of Ireland was still part of the United Kingdom of Great Britain and Ireland, and subject to the rule of the Westminster Parliament. However, following centuries of discontent in Ireland, Sinn Fein had led a rebellion at Easter 1916, centred on Dublin, and aiming at the overthrow of British rule.

b British troops put this down, amid much damage and bloodshed, and several of the Sinn Fein leaders were court-martialled and shot for treason. This caused great bitterness against the British in Ireland, and helped the Sinn Fein cause.

c however, Sinn Fein did not want violence, so in 1918 their MPs simply refused to come

Fig. 9   Britain's coal industry was in a poor state between the wars. Mining methods were backward, and most coal was still 'won' by hand, as here.

Fig. 10   The growth of suburban housing. A garage for the family car was a 'must'.

to Westminster, but set up their own assembly (the Dail) in Dublin, ignoring the British administration, with Eamon de Valera, a survivor of 1916, as President.

8 However, fighting ('the troubles') soon broke out:

a in 1919 a party of Irish National Volunteers (later known as the IRA, Irish Republican Army) ambushed and shot two members of the RIC (Royal Irish Constabulary). This marked the start of a long and bitter struggle.

b Michael Collins led the IRA in a successful guerilla war of ambushes and assassinations, while the British became increasingly brutal in reply. Troops were sent to Ireland, and the RIC were assisted by the 'Black and Tans' (recently demobilised soldiers wearing black belts with their khaki uniforms) and the Auxiliaries (ex-officers).

c these forces killed prisoners and suspects ruthlessly. One of their commanders said later that they were employed to 'murder, rob, loot and burn up the innocent because they could not catch a few guilty men on the run'. When the facts became known in Britain, public opinion was horrified.

d yet reaching a settlement proved difficult. Many of Lloyd George's Coalition Govern-ment were not prepared to see Protestant Ulster pass under the rule of the Catholic south of Ireland, while for Sinn Fein the ideal was a united Ireland.

e however, Lloyd George bluffed the leading Irish negotiators, Michael Collins and Arthur Griffith, into agreeing to a partition of Ireland in 1921 by a threat of all-out war if they refused to accept.

9 The settlement. This was reached in December 1921, and came into force the following year:

a the Irish Free State was to consist of the twenty-six southern counties, with full self-government within the Commonwealth.

b the six counties of Ulster remained under British rule, with MPs at Westminster, and their own Parliament at Stormont for local matters.

c Britain retained three 'treaty ports' in the Free State, Queenstown, Berehaven, and Lough Swilly, for the use of the Royal Navy.

d De Valera and a minority of the Dail would not accept this settlement. Griffith succeeded de Valera as President, and de Valera and his followers now began a civil war against his former Sinn Fein colleagues, which lasted until 1923. By then Collins, who supported the treaty, had been shot by its opponents, and Griffith had died from exhaustion. However, the treaty's supporters, with a new leader, Cosgrave, won the struggle.

Fig. 11   Irish Free State troops in action, Dublin, 1922.

10 Foreign affairs – see Ch. 3.

11 The Empire's position after 1918:

a after the Versailles Settlement, the British Empire, or Commonwealth as it was soon to be called, was at its largest, as many of Germany's former colonies had passed to Britain and her Dominions. The Empire also seemed stronger than ever before.

b many of the colonies and dominions had supported Britain well in the war, e.g. Canada, Australia and New Zealand. Yet their part in the war had encouraged such countries to think of themselves as nations in their own right, fully equal to and independent of Britain.

c also, wartime difficulties had led some parts of the Empire, such as India, to become less dependent on imports from Britain, e.g. cotton cloth, and to look elsewhere for suppliers, or develop their own industries. Many people, especially in the British Conservative Party, thought that the Empire might be made stronger and more united by introducing trading agreements along the lines of imperial preference, i.e. allowing imports of Commonwealth goods into Britain at lower duties than those that would be imposed on foreign goods, if and when Britain returned to a policy of protection. However, the world-wide depression made such plans difficult to put into effect (see Ch. 3). For instance, a Commonwealth country wishing to develop its own manufactures might put tariffs on imports of such goods from Britain.

d however, except in Egypt and India, there was no clear sign of the break-up of the Empire that was to come after the Second World War.

12 Egypt. Britain had occupied Egypt (then in theory part of the Turkish Empire) since 1882 and the Suez Canal was thought to be vital to Empire trade and defence. Though Britain controlled and defended Egypt, in fact she never claimed it as part of her Empire.

During the First World War, Britain declared a 'protectorate' over Egypt, but when the war ended the Nationalist Wafd party demanded independence. This Britain proclaimed in 1922, but British troops stayed (supposedly for the defence of the canal) and Britain kept control. Thus Egyptian discontent at British rule increased, and relations between the two countries grew worse.

13 India. The 'Empire of India' was formed of a large number of states, some under British rule, some ruled by Indian Princes. One of George V's titles was 'Emperor of India' and the British Viceroy in the capital, Delhi, still had considerable powers, although steps had been taken to allow local self-government. The two main political parties were the Congress Party (mainly Hindu) and the Moslem League.

There were many disturbances in India at the end of the war, with religious riots between Hindus and Moslems. Much anti-British feeling was caused by the massacre at Amritsar in 1919, when General Dyer's troops opened fire on a dense crowd and killed nearly four hundred Indians. Later he ordered that Indians passing the spot where a white lady missionary had been beaten must crawl. Dyer was recalled and had to resign, but the damage had been done. Many moderate Indians, like Gandhi, now became determined on self-rule.

14 Causes of Lloyd George's fall from power. By late 1922 Lloyd George was in a difficult spot. In pre-war days he had been hailed as a great social reformer, the friend of the working classes and the poor, a champion of freedom. In 1918 the country had looked forward to a great future under his leadership, and it was said he could have been Prime Minister for life. Since then his reputation had suffered badly:

a 'homes for heroes' had not been built. There was a desperate housing shortage instead.

b 'jobs for all' had given way to high unemployment.

c the 'Geddes Axe' had fallen on education.

d he had allowed terrorist methods to be used by the British forces in Ireland, while later offending many of his Unionist allies by allowing home rule for the south.

e he had sold honours for money payments and controlled a large fund which was supposed to be for the benefit of the Liberal Party, but which he refused to hand over. Thus his honesty was questioned.

f through spending so much time abroad dealing with foreign affairs, he neglected to attend the House of Commons as much as he should.

g finally, the Chanak Crisis (see Ch. 3) was blamed on him.

15 The showdown came when he decided to call a general election in late 1922. A meeting of Conservative MPs was held at the Carlton Club on 19 October. By now Bonar Law had resigned as Conservative leader, and Austen Chamberlain had taken his place. Many Conservatives felt that Lloyd George was leading the Coalition to disaster, and Stanley Baldwin persuaded Law to attend the meeting and attack the continuance of the Conservatives in it. Law and Baldwin both spoke effectively, and the meeting voted 187 to 87 in their support.

Lloyd George resigned, and at the general election Bonar Law, who had taken Chamberlain's place as leader, led the Conservatives to a sweeping victory:

Conservatives 347 seats
Labour 142 seats
Lloyd George Liberals 57 seats
Asquith Liberals 60 seats

Thus a Conservative government was formed, with Law as Prime Minister at first.

D The Conservative Government of 1922-4

1 Law formed a government without several important Conservatives such as Austen Chamberlain, A. J. Balfour and Lord Birkenhead, all of whom had supported the Coalition and so felt they could not join the new Ministry, though Lord Curzon agreed to serve as Foreign Secretary. Therefore Stanley Baldwin became Chancellor of the Exchequer. Then in May 1923, Law, ill with cancer, resigned. Baldwin, rather than the unpopular Curzon, became Prime Minister in his place.

2 Yet in November 1923 Baldwin dissolved Parliament and a general election was fought in December. Baldwin gave as his reason for this action that he felt unemployment could not be tackled without tariffs, and in the election campaign of 1922 Bonar Law had promised these would not be introduced without a further general election on the issue. Both Labour and the Liberals (with Asquith and Lloyd George now reunited) campaigned to keep Britain a free trade country, and said that tariffs would mean higher prices, especially of food. The result was a disaster for the Conservatives:

Conservatives 258 seats
Labour 191 seats
Liberals 158 seats

3 Baldwin did not resign however, until January 1924, when his government was defeated in the Commons on a motion of no confidence. Labour, though only the second largest Party in the Commons, now took office for the first time.

Fig. 12 Stanley Baldwin (1867-1947) dominated British politics between the wars. People, even his opponents in the Labour Party, felt they could trust 'honest Stan'. Thus he was able to keep men such as Lloyd George and Churchill out of office, and proved a great electoral asset to the Conservative Party. He was careful to pay great attention to Commons business, and was determined to preserve national unity. Thus, except for the Trades Disputes Act of 1927, he refused to take any steps against the trade unions. By 1935, however, when he became Prime Minister for the last time, he was ageing, and proved no match for Hitler and Mussolini.

E The First Labour Government, 1924

1 Domestic policies. Ramsay MacDonald became Prime Minister and Foreign Secretary, with Philip Snowden as Chancellor of the Exchequer. Heavily outnumbered in the Commons, the government could not introduce any really Socialist measures, but aimed to show that Labour was fit to govern:

a the government received little support from the trade unions, and when faced by strikes, prepared to use the Emergency Powers Act which allowed troops to be called in to keep essential services running.

b one of the more successful Ministers was John Wheatley, whose Housing Act of 1924 offered an increased subsidy of £9 a year for forty years for each house built. This was intended to especially encourage council house building for rental.

c C. P. Trevelyan, Minister of Education, repaired some of the damage done by the 'Geddes Axe', by doing away with some economies in secondary education.

2 Foreign policy—see Ch. 3.

3 Fall of the first Labour Government:

a MacDonald's relations with Russia had been attacked by the Conservatives, who seized upon the Campbell case as a weapon against the government. J. R. Campbell, editor of the Communist 'Workers' Weekly', was charged with inciting soldiers to mutiny by urging them not to act as strike breakers.

b during the summer recess of Parliament the Attorney-General dropped the case as he felt no jury would convict. However, when Parliament met in the autumn, the Liberals joined with the Conservatives to pass a vote of censure in the Commons on this issue, saying that the Attorney-General had acted from political motives.

c thus the government had to resign, and a general election followed in October.

4 A few days before the voting, the 'Daily Mail' published the 'Zinoviev letter'. This, a probable forgery, was supposed to be from a member of the Russian Government, Zinoviev, to the British Communist Party, urging them to support the Labour Government's proposed treaty with Russia, as it would help Communists to gain power in Britain. This, the Conservatives claimed, showed that the country was not safe under Labour. The Labour Party blamed their defeat largely on the Zinoviev affair. The result of the election was:

Conservatives 415 seats

Labour 152 seats

Liberals 42 seats

In fact, the Labour vote had increased by over a million. The biggest losers were the Liberals, who have never really recovered from this defeat in 1924, and have remained the smallest of the three main parties ever since.

Fig. 13 Ramsay MacDonald (1866-1937) was a brilliant speaker with a winning personality, who must take much of the credit for the rapid growth of the Labour Party and its electoral victories in the 1920s. Like Baldwin, he was keen on national unity. Yet his decision to form a 'National' Government in 1931 was considered a great betrayal by most of his party, which expelled him, and he had to rely on Conservative support to stay in office. By 1935, when he resigned, he was under great mental strain, and incapable of handling the country's affairs efficiently. After his death he, like Baldwin, was forgotten or held in contempt, but by the 1960s opinion was changing, and one famous historian referred to him as 'the greatest leader labour has had'.

F The 'Golden Age' of Baldwin, 1924-9

This, Baldwin's second Ministry, marked the end of twenty troubled years in domestic and foreign affairs, and was to be followed by many more years of grave economic and foreign problems, so that it now seems to be (apart from the General Strike of 1926) a calm interlude in a stormy century. After three general elections and four Prime Ministers in just over two years, the electorate welcomed what Baldwin himself called his policy of 'safety first'.

1 Domestic reforms:

a these were years of quiet achievement. The Conservative Coalitionists who had refused to serve under Baldwin in 1923 now agreed to do so. Thus Baldwin reunited his party, with Austen Chamberlain as Foreign Secretary and Winston Churchill as Chancellor of the Exchequer. Neville Chamberlain, Austen's half-brother, proved a successful Minister of Health.

Fig. 14   Neville Chamberlain (1869-1940) relaxes, 1933. He never really mastered the House of Commons as Baldwin did, and could not tolerate opposition. Thus he offended the Labour Party and seemed to treat them with contempt. On becoming Prime Minister in 1937, he was convinced that he could reach an honourable settlement with Hitler and Mussolini, but surrounded himself with 'yes-men' as advisers.

b yet, at the Exchequer, Churchill was a misfit. In his 1925 budget, in an effort to restore foreign confidence in the pound, he put Britain back on the gold standard. This meant that the pound was backed by a fixed value in gold. Unfortunately, the pound was valued too highly at $4.80. This made British exports dear, and so other countries could not afford to buy as much from Britain.

c the 1925 Widows, Orphans and Old Age Contributory Pensions Act. This was a new pension scheme, introduced by Neville Chamberlain. All people covered by National Health insurance now had to pay contributions which provided pensions for widows and their dependants, and old age pensions at 65 (instead of at 70 as under previous acts).

d in 1926 the government set up the Central Electricity Board (now the Central Electricity Generating Board). This was to build a national grid, or network of power lines, to cover Britain and allow electricity to be produced and distributed on a large scale. Also the Board was to help to standardize voltages throughout Britain. The Board was to buy electricity from the power stations and sell it to users via the national grid. This was completed by 1934.

e in 1926 the British Broadcasting Corporation was formed, by Royal Charter, and given a monopoly of radio broadcasting in Britain. Its first director-general was John Reith. Under him the BBC set a standard of honesty, fairness and good quality programmes that other countries envied. News broadcasts had to be impartial, not favouring the government or any one political party. To balance the entertainment, such as music, which was transmitted there were educational broadcasts and talks. Reith believed that radio must be used to help improve people's minds and increase their knowledge.

f in 1928 the Equal Franchise Act gave women the vote on the same footing as men, i.e. all over 21 were now allowed to vote.

g in 1929 Neville Chamberlain introduced his major reform, the Local Government Act. It did two main things:

Agricultural buildings and land were completely derated, i.e. had to pay no rates to the local councils, while industrial premises, such as factories and railways, only had to pay one-quarter of their former rates. This measure was designed to help industry and agriculture in difficult times.

The Poor Law Unions and Boards of Guardians were abolished, and their duties taken over by Public Assistance Committees of the County and Borough Councils. This meant that the cost of Poor Relief was spread over larger areas, which made things less difficult for unemployment black spots.

2 Industrial unrest and the General Strike of 1926:

a the problem of the coal mining industry had been shelved, not solved, and in 1925 Baldwin prevented a miners' strike by agreeing to pay the mine owners a subsidy for one year to help them maintain the level of miners' wages. At the same time, he set up a Royal Commission under Sir Herbert Samuel to study the problem.

b in March 1926 the Commission, in a long report, recommended many changes but said that wages must be reduced, at least for a time. Both sides in the industry would not budge. The miners' leaders, A. J. Cook and Herbert Smith, stuck to their slogan of 'Not a minute on the day, not a penny off the pay', while the mine owners' only solution to the industry's difficulties was a proposed one-eighth cut in wages and a one-hour increase in the working day.

c meanwhile, Baldwin had used the year's time bought by the mining subsidy to prepare for a general strike if one came. Plans were made to divide the country into ten regions, each under a commissioner, who would rule under the Emergency Powers Act if necessary. Food supplies were collected, and plans made for their transportation.

d the TUC, on the other hand, made no serious plans for a general strike until a few days before it called one. It trusted that the government could be forced to give way by bluff.

e the miners were locked out on 1 May 1926.

The TUC continued to negotiate with the government, but Baldwin called this off, using as an excuse the refusal of the 'Daily Mail' printers to print an article attacking the idea of a general strike.

f the leaders of the TUC called for a general strike to begin on 3 May. This was to support the miners. Many workers in transport and industry stopped work. In fact, the strike was not 'general'. Essential services, such as electricity, gas and water supplies, were kept going by non-strikers. As no newspapers were printed, the government issued one of its own, the 'British Gazette', edited by Winston Churchill. The spread of radio helped the government to keep in touch with the people. Baldwin refused to do anything to inflame the dispute.

g after ten days the TUC leaders, as the strike seemed to be getting them nowhere, ordered their members back to work. They used Sir Herbert Samuel's offer to mediate (which was rejected by the miners) as an excuse.

Fig. 15 Fixing barbed wire round the bonnet of a bus in London during the General Strike of 1926. The fact that volunteers drove buses, cars and lorries meant that the stoppage of rail transport was not as crippling as it would formerly have been.

3 Effects of the General Strike:

a the miners stayed out for another six months, then were forced by starvation to go back to work on the employers' terms.

b the strike's failure was a blow to the trade union movement. It had cost their funds £4,000,000 and union membership fell steadily to just over four million in 1933.

c there was some victimisation of strikers. The government passed the Trades Disputes Act in 1927. This said that sympathetic strikes, as the General Strike had been, were illegal, also that civil service trade unions were not to belong to the TUC.

d in addition, the Trade Union Act of 1913 was amended. In future, the 'political levy' (money paid by a trade unionist with his union subscription for a political fund, which usually helped the Labour Party) would only be paid if a member of a union signed a form saying he wished to pay it. This was called 'contracting in'. It made it easier to avoid payment and was a blow at the Labour Party.

4 Foreign policies – see Ch. 3.

5 The Commonwealth:

a in 1926, at the Imperial Conference of Prime Ministers, Britain recognised that the Dominions were in fact fully independent of the British Government, with the Crown as the only link between them and Britain.

b in 1926 Baldwin sent Lord Irwin (later Viscount Halifax) to India as Viceroy. Irwin believed in eventual Dominion status for India, and in 1927 Sir John Simon was sent to India as head of a commission to recommend on India's future government.

6 Fall of the government. In May 1929 Baldwin called a general election. The result showed that the country was very much divided. Labour gained 288 seats, and the Conservatives (who polled more votes) 260. The Liberals, led by Lloyd George, received nearly 5½ million votes, but only 59 seats. Baldwin resigned before Parliament met, and George V sent for Ramsay MacDonald to form his second Labour Government.

G The Second Labour Government, 1929–31

1 This time MacDonald did not act as Foreign Secretary. He appointed Arthur Henderson to the post. Once again Snowden was Chancellor of the Exchequer. This government included the first woman Cabinet Minister, Margaret Bondfield.

2 Domestic reforms. Before its fall in 1931 the government managed to introduce some changes, but was prevented, because it was in a minority in the Commons, from making others:

a in 1930 the Coal Mines Act reduced the miners' working day from eight hours to seven and a half. Also, mine owners were to limit output according to district quotas and minimum prices were fixed.

b Herbert Morrison introduced the bill which was to set up the London Passenger Transport Board after the government had fallen from office.

c Greenwood's Housing Act of 1930 encouraged local councils to clear slums, and build new houses or flats in their place. In the economy drive after 1931, when public spending was cut, many such schemes suffered. Yet progress was made. Some towns, e.g. Leeds, cleared slums and built blocks of flats in their place. Others built new housing estates on their outskirts, e.g. Manchester's Wythenshawe estate.

d attempts to raise the school leaving age to 15 (from 14) and to modify the Trades Disputes Act of 1927 came to nothing.

3 Foreign policies – see Ch. 3.

4 The Commonwealth:

a India. The report of the Simon Commission in 1930 promised local self-government to the Indian Provinces, and some say for Indians in the central government of their country, but was greeted with suspicion by the Indians themselves.

b The Statute of Westminster in 1931 gave full legal force to the Declaration of 1926 which had recognised the independence of the Dominions.

5 Economic difficulties:

a the great slump of 1929 onwards (see Ch. 3) was disastrous for Britain. Foreign trade fell, partly because other countries could not afford to buy British goods, partly because they increased tariff barriers to protect their own industries.

b unemployment rose from one million in 1929 to three million in 1932.

c foreign investors began to withdraw large sums of money which had been invested in London. British gold reserves fell, as did the value of the pound.

d by 1931 these problems were beyond the power of the minority Labour Government to tackle. Then in the summer two committees set up by the government reported and added further to the alarm.

e the Macmillan Committee on Finance and Industry pointed out that Britain's trade with other countries was failing to balance, i.e. that she was importing more than she could pay for by exports, and her 'invisible income' from such things as shipping and banking had fallen with the depression.

f the May Committee forecast a deficit on the budget of £120,000,000 and recommended pay cuts for the forces, civil servants, teachers and police, as well as a 20% reduction in unemployment benefit.

6 The Cabinet was split on the May proposals, and so MacDonald, in August, handed in his government's resignation, then astonished the Labour movement by announcing, on the same day, that he was forming a 'National' Government, to include Conservative and Liberal leaders, with the aim of tackling the economic crisis.

If he expected the Labour Party to support him over this, he miscalculated badly. Only a handful of his Cabinet colleagues and Labour MPs followed him. All were expelled by the Labour Party, which went into opposition. However, a new Cabinet including MacDonald as Prime Minister, Snowden as Chancellor of the Exchequer, Baldwin and Chamberlain from the Conservatives and Sir Herbert Samuel from the Liberals took office.

H The National Government, 1931–9

1 The general election of 1931:

a Snowden at once brought in an emergency budget in September, which increased taxation, and cut salaries of public employees and unemployment benefit (though not as severely as recommended by the May Committee). Yet pressure on the pound and gold reserves continued, especially after sailors of the Royal Navy at Invergordon mutinied against cuts in their pay. Thus the government was forced to come off the gold standard and the pound was devalued to a much lower level.

b MacDonald now decided on a general election, calling for a 'doctor's mandate' for the National Government from the voters, i.e. to put into effect unpleasant measures to prevent complete economic collapse. Labour could put forward no satisfactory solution to the country's problems. The result was a massive win for the government:

> National 521 seats
> Labour 52 seats
> Liberal 33 seats

2 Economic policies:

a recovery was slow. It came finally because the threat from Hitler's Germany caused Britain to rearm in the late 1930s, thus creating tens of thousands of new jobs, especially in arms and aircraft factories.
John Maynard Keynes in his book 'The General Theory of Employment, Interest and Money' pointed out a cure for unemployment. Governments, he said, should spend more, not less, in times of slump, e.g. on public works such as roads and bridges. They should run up a budget deficit in order to do so. This would create more jobs.
At the time, however, the government still believed that, apart from balancing the budget, there was little they could do to cure unemployment. Yet some steps were taken.

b Britain abandoned free trade and returned to protection. By the Import Duties Act of 1932 a tariff of 10% (later increased to 20%) could be imposed on imports from abroad.

c in 1932 at Ottawa Britain made a series of agreements with Commonwealth countries on 'imperial preference' i.e. lower duties on trade among the Commonwealth countries than on goods from outsiders.

d a Special Areas Act was passed in 1934. Under it and later acts, the government spent money to encourage new industries into the worst-hit areas of unemployment, but not enough was done.

e individual industries.

Cotton was badly hit and production and exports fell steadily. A 'Spindles Board' was set up by the government to encourage mills to scrap machinery or even to close.

Steel was protected by a high tariff. The British Iron and Steel Federation was set up to limit price competition between firms in Britain. Thus steel recovered fairly well.

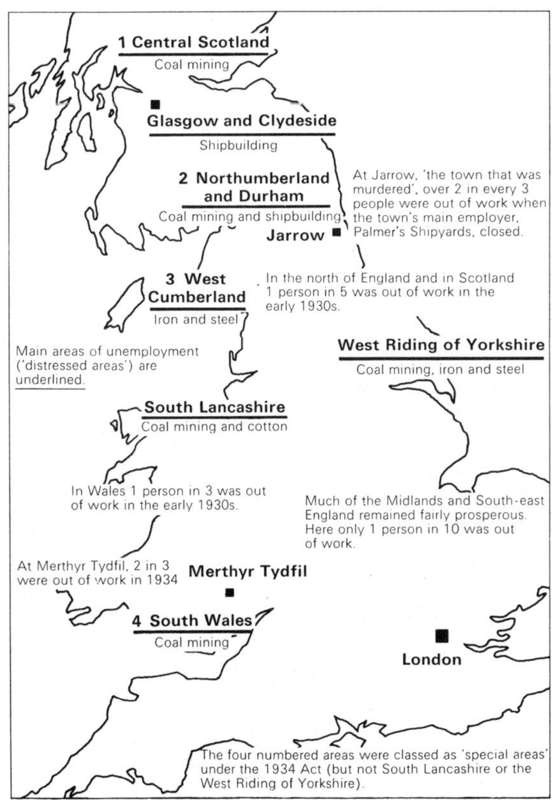

Fig. 16 'Depressed areas' in the 1930s. These were the centres of the old staple British industries of coal, cotton, steel and shipbuilding.

Coal production fell, then recovered, helped by the 1930 Mines Act.

Shipbuilding never recovered from the slump, despite government help to complete the liner 'Queen Mary', and the rearmament programme.

f the government imposed some tariffs on imports of food from foreign countries, though food from the Commonwealth was duty-free. However, as tariffs put up food prices in the shops, they were unpopular with the public, and so imports of some foreign foods, e.g. bacon from Denmark, were restricted to a fixed amount or 'quota'.

By the Agricultural Marketing Act of 1933 food producers were encouraged to set up marketing boards to help them sell their produce and cut out wasteful competition and price-cutting. The most famous example is the Milk Marketing Board. This offered farmers a guaranteed price for their milk, collected it and sold it.

Thus, by 1939 when the Second World War broke out, farming had regained some of its prosperity, though at a cost to the government of £100,000,000 a year.

3 Regional differences. Many writers between the wars remarked that there seemed to be two Britains:

a in the depressed areas unemployment was to many a 'way of life' (see fig. 7).

b yet for many others, especially in the prosperous south-east and midlands where new industries were growing, such as manufacture of motor vehicles and electrical goods and machinery, the years 1918–39 saw a steady improvement in living standards. The average worker was probably about a third better off in 1939 than in 1914, as wages had risen more than prices.

c though slums remained, many new houses were built. As the 1930s wore on, there was a boom in private house building, usually houses for sale. (There were several reasons for this. Land prices were low and building materials, e.g. imported timber, were cheap. Wages in the building industry were low. Mortgages at low rates of interest, perhaps 3%, were easily obtainable.) Thus by 1939 several hundred thousand houses a year were being built.

d food was cheap, mainly because of cheap imports. More people could afford to take a holiday away from home. Entertainment became more widespread through the radio and cinema. Housework became easier as the use of domestic appliances, such as the vacuum cleaner, increased. By today's standards taxes were low, and there was no VAT.

4 Rearmament. As it became clear that Hitler's Germany was a threat to Britain, the government launched a massive rearmament programme in the late 1930s (see Ch. 3). Hundreds of thousands of people found jobs making aircraft, ships and equipment for the army. Other industries, such as steel and coal, were stimulated in turn. Thus by 1939 unemployment was down to one million, though even in 1940, when Britain was fighting for her life, there were many out of work.

5 Foreign policies – see Ch. 3.

6 The Commonwealth. The Government of India Act, 1935, granted more self-government in local affairs to parts of India, but important matters such as foreign affairs and defence were still to be controlled by the Viceroy. This did not satisfy Indian leaders such as Gandhi.

7 Britain made another treaty with Egypt in 1936, again promising to withdraw troops eventually, but in fact the British retained control.

8 Ireland, led by de Valera, declared herself independent as 'Eire' in 1937.

I Personalities

1 Ramsay MacDonald remained as Prime Minister until 1935, but in fact the Conservatives were in power, as they held the vast majority of 'National' seats in the Commons. By 1935, however, he had aged rapidly, and handed over to Baldwin as Prime Minister before the general election of that year. In the election, the government scored another victory, though not as big as in 1931:

National 432 seats
Labour 154 seats
Liberal 20 seats

2 King Edward VIII, formerly Edward Prince of Wales, succeeded his father, George V, in January 1936, to reign for less than one year. When the King made it clear that he intended to marry Mrs Wallis Simpson, an American divorcee, Baldwin, backed by Labour and Liberal leaders, as well as the Dominion Prime Ministers, made it clear that he could not do so and remain King.

Therefore on 11 December Edward VIII abdicated in favour of his younger brother, the Duke of York, who became King as George VI. Edward took the title of Duke of Windsor, and went into exile.

3 Baldwin himself resigned after the Coronation of King George VI and Queen Elizabeth in 1937, giving Neville Chamberlain his long-awaited chance as Prime Minister. By now Germany was clearly a growing menace, and most of Chamberlain's energies were directed into trying to reach a settlement with Hitler.

Fig. 17   Launching of HMS Ark Royal at Birkenhead, 1937, part of the rearmament programme.

A The Powers after 1919

1 Britain had three main aims in foreign affairs:

a as a trading nation, war would be damaging by cutting her off from sources of raw materials and from markets for finished goods. Some of this damage could be permanent and so Britain wanted to keep the peace whenever possible. The terrible losses of men in the First World War, and fears that a future war would be even more terrible, strengthened this feeling for peace.

b she needed to protect trade routes and the sea routes to the Empire had to be kept open.

c traditionally she had favoured the 'balance of power' in Europe, i.e. preventing any one country from becoming so strong as to dominate the continent.

2 Britain differed from her ally, France, in her attitude towards Germany. As the German Fleet was no more (its crews had scuttled it at Scapa Flow in 1919) Britain believed that Germany could no longer be a threat. (The idea of a strong bombing force of aircraft had hardly been born.) As she had been a good customer Britain wanted Germany to recover quickly from the war.

Fig. 18 Winston Churchill, 1874-1965. Few heeded his warnings in the late 1930s that Hitler was bent on war, and that Britain must prepare.

3 Regarding war debts, Britain proposed in 1922 a general cancellation of all such debts among the former Allies, but the USA and France rejected this. Thus Britain contented herself with saying that she would only collect enough from her debtors to pay off what she owed the USA.

4 In 1919 Britain supplied the 'Whites' in Russia, who were fighting the 'Red' (Communist) Government, with £100,000,000 worth of war material, such as surplus tanks and guns, and sent troops to Baku and Murmansk in Russia to guard stores. Winston Churchill, Secretary of State for War, strongly supported this policy as did many Conservatives, in the hope of overthrowing Bolshevism. Lloyd George, the Prime Minister, was not so keen, and there was much opposition from the Labour Party and trade unions to this policy of 'intervention'.

By late 1919 the Reds were obviously winning, and Britain withdrew her troops from Russia, where her actions left a feeling of bitterness.

5 The next year, in 1920, when war broke out between Russia and Poland over their frontier, the British Government was prepared to send arms to the Poles. However, London dockers refused to load such a cargo on to the cargo ship 'Jolly George' and the trade unions threatened a general strike. Lloyd George was glad to back down and cancel the aid to Poland.

6 France:

a though on the winning side in 1918, France had suffered terrible losses in men and still dreaded the thought of another attack from Germany, who, despite losses of territory and population by the Treaty of Versailles, still had a much bigger population than France. Also, Germany would have a far higher output of coal and steel for making weapons once recovered fully from the war.

b thus France had tried and failed at Versailles to crush Germany once and for all, by demanding that Germany lose all her territory to the west of the Rhine. Britain had talked the French out of this by promising a guarantee to protect French territory against German attack by both Britain and the USA. However, the USA rejected the Versailles

Treaty and would not guarantee France. Britain refused to do so on her own, except in the event of a German army actually invading France, which would have been too late from the French point of view.

c thus France now refused to disarm, and tried to keep Germany weak by demanding full and prompt payment of reparations, especially under the right-wing government of Poincaré. This attitude led many in Britain to favour Germany, as they thought France was being unreasonable. France entered into a series of alliances with Belgium, Poland, Czechoslovakia, Rumania and Yugoslavia.

7 Germany. There was much resentment in Germany against the Treaty of Versailles. As both Germany and Russia were outcasts after 1918 as far as Britain and France were concerned, it was natural that the former two countries should come together. This they did, making a treaty at Rapallo in 1922 which cancelled reparations and debts between them. Secret agreements then and later between the two allowed Germany to develop tanks and military aircraft (both forbidden under the Versailles Treaty) in Russia.

8 Russia was still very weak after the defeat she had suffered in the First World War, the effects of revolution, and the civil war which had followed it. Thus she was to concentrate on internal recovery rather than international affairs in the 1920s.

Though Ramsay MacDonald's Labour Government of 1924 fully recognised Soviet Russia, nothing came of his plan to improve trade with her. One stumbling-block was the question of Russia's debts to Britain, debts which had been incurred by the Tsar's Governments before the revolution. Russia's Communist rulers refused to repay these on the grounds that they were loans to the Tsar in person.

Many in Britain, especially in the Conservative Party, were deeply suspicious of Russia, especially because of the Comintern (short for Communist International). This was an international organisation, founded in Moscow in 1919, to spread the Communist revolution to all countries.

9 The USA:

a there was strong feeling of 'isolationism' in the USA between the two World Wars. This meant that many Americans felt that the USA should cut herself off from European affairs and never again become involved in a European war. Thus the Senate refused to ratify the Versailles Treaty, the USA did not join the League of Nations, and President Wilson was defeated in the presidential election of 1920.

b one positive achievement was the Washington Naval Treaty of 1922, when Britain, the USA and Japan agreed to limit their battleships (then the most powerful sea weapons) to a ratio of 5:5:3 (i.e. for every 5 the Americans had or built, Britain could have 5 and the Japanese 3).

c at the same time, under Dominion pressure, and fearing to be drawn into a possible future war with the USA, Britain abandoned her alliance with Japan, which had lasted since 1902. Instead, the British promised the Japanese not to develop a naval base at Hong Kong, and the Americans promised not to develop one in the Philippines.

Fig. 19   President Woodrow Wilson, 1856-1924.

10 Turkey. By the Treaty of Sèvres (1920) Turkey had not only lost all her Empire in Asia, but also much of Turkey proper was to pass under the control of France, Italy and Greece, including the capital, Constantinople, itself:

Fig. 20   Refugees flee from the burning part of Smyrna during the Turkish crisis of 1922.

Fig. 21   French troops occupy the Ruhr in 1923.

a there was great resentment against this settlement in Turkey, which led to the rise of a new leader, Mustapha Kemal (later called Kemal Ataturk), who proclaimed a Republic and moved the capital to Ankara. He then set out to modernise Turkey and overthrow the Sèvres settlement.

b France and Italy withdrew from Turkey. The Greeks fought back, however, and Kemal routed them.

c Turkish troops advanced on Constantinople, and faced a British force under General Harington who garrisoned an outpost of the neutral zone at Chanak. Lloyd George ordered Harington to attack the Turks if they did not withdraw. Harington ignored this order, the Turks advanced no further, and so a peaceful settlement was possible.

d this was reached by the Treaty of Lausanne (1923) which restored Turkey to her present boundaries, including the return of Constantinople.

e Lloyd George came under heavy attack in Britain for almost taking the country into another war, and the Conservatives decided he was too dangerous to support any longer (see Ch. 2). Yet he had, after all, only prepared to fight to support part of the Versailles Settlement.

B Events, 1923–4

1 The Reparations Crisis. The actual figure of reparations to be paid by Germany to the Allies was left to be fixed by a 'Reparations Commission'. In 1921 this body decided on a figure of £6,600,000,000 to be paid in gold by yearly instalments:

a though the Allies believed they had the right to compensation for their losses in the war, they failed to realise that Germany could only raise this money by increasing her exports, and thus competing with the Allies for foreign markets. This meant intense competition for e.g. the British coal industry.

b when in 1923 the Germans said they could not pay the current instalment, French and Belgian troops occupied the industrial Ruhr area of Germany. The French hoped to take over the area's coal mines and steel works to make up for the loss of reparations. However, the German workers went on strike, supported by their government.

c the temporary loss of the Ruhr, which produced most of Germany's coal and iron, was disastrous for the German economy. To balance the budget, the government printed vast quantities of paper money, and the result was a spiral of inflation. By the end of 1923 the mark was almost worthless. It cost hundreds of millions to post a letter, for instance. This had very serious effects in Germany (see Ch. 5).

d this was the position facing Gustav Stresemann when he became German Chancellor in 1923. He realised that Germany must reach a settlement with the French, and so called off the strikes in the Ruhr and promised to pay what Germany could afford in reparations.

e the Allies, especially Britain, wanted to reach a settlement with Germany. This feeling was helped by the coming to power of Ramsay MacDonald's Labour Government (he took a keen interest in foreign affairs) and the fall of Poincaré's Government in France. The new Prime Minister there, Herriot, and his Foreign Secretary, Briand, both favoured moderation towards Germany.

f the USA agreed to mediate, and so in 1924 the Dawes Plan (named after the American General who drew it up) was adopted.

France and Belgium withdrew their troops from the Ruhr. The Reichsmark was to be revalued at twenty to the pound. Reparations were to be reduced, and made payable in German currency instead of gold. Germany was to receive a foreign loan to help re-start her economy. The plan was successful. German industry boomed, though dependent on short-term loans from the USA.

2 The Geneva Protocol. This was an attempt to make the League of Nations effective. Ramsay MacDonald himself went to the League's headquarters at Geneva and supported the plan.

Disputes between states were to be subject to arbitration by the League. Any state branded as an aggressor, or refusing arbitration, was to be subject to economic sanctions (e.g. trade bans) and possibly the use of force by all members of the League. Even internal disputes, for instance over a minority race inside a country, were to be subject to this ruling, and the Council of the League no longer had to be unanimous, as was then the case, in recommending action.

However, the British Dominions opposed the Protocol and in 1925 the British Government under Stanley Baldwin rejected the idea.

C Years of Hope, 1925–9

1 These were at the time years of great optimism. Britain, with Austen Chamberlain as Foreign Secretary; France, represented by Aristide Briand; and Germany under Stresemann worked well together, and the possibility of another war seemed far off. In fact the British Government adopted the 'ten-year rule' which meant that as far as British forces were concerned there was held to be no chance of a major war for another ten years. This enabled spending on them to be trimmed accordingly. Each year until the mid-thirties this rule was readopted.

The only cloud on Britain's horizon seemed to be Soviet Russia. The Zinoviev letter scare of 1924 convinced many that Russia was intent on starting a revolution in Britain, and the

Conservatives dropped the proposed Anglo-Russian Treaty on their return to power in 1924. In 1927 police raided the offices of Arcos, the Russian trading mission in London. Though no evidence of a Communist plot was found, Britain broke off diplomatic relations with Russia. (Labour restored them on taking office in 1929.)

2 The Locarno Treaties of 1925. These followed negotiations at the Swiss resort of Locarno. One treaty guaranteed the Franco-German and Belgian-German frontiers against aggression by either Germany or France. This was signed by France, Britain, Germany, Belgium and Italy.

Germany agreed to submit disputes over her borders with Poland and Czechoslovakia to arbitration (but did not guarantee to respect these borders).

France signed treaties offering to help defend both Poland and Czechoslovakia against attack by Germany.

To many at the time, Locarno seemed a great step forward. For the first time, Germany freely accepted the western frontier imposed on her by the 'Diktat' of Versailles. Yet Germany had not accepted her eastern frontiers, and the fact that the Locarno Treaties were signed at all seemed to show that the Versailles Settlement was not enough in itself, and that the League alone could not be relied on to keep the peace.

3 The Kellogg Pact of 1928 (Treaty of Paris). This was the work of the American Secretary of State, Kellogg, and Briand of France. Altogether, sixty-five countries signed the treaty, which bound them not to go to war except in self-defence. This looked impressive. The number of countries signing was more than had ever signed a single treaty before. Yet 'self-defence' could be used by an aggressor to cover almost any warlike action.

4 The Young Plan, 1929. This was adopted at The Hague, and was named after the American chairman of a committee formed to consider reparations. It was agreed that Germany was to take control of her reparations payments, which were to be reduced slightly, and continue until 1988.

The Allies further demonstrated their trust in Germany by withdrawing their forces from the Rhineland, five years before the date laid down at Versailles. Thus it seemed that peace was secured.

Yet by the end of the year the great slump had begun, and the world was on the path leading to the Second World War.

D The League of Nations in the Twenties

1 Organisation. Various departments of the League were responsible for e.g. the mandated territories (Germany's former colonies and parts of the former Turkish Empire which had been shared out among the Allies), the protection of national minorities, and the administration of the Free City of Danzig and the Saar.

There was an International Court of Justice at The Hague.

An International Labour Organisation (ILO) aimed at improving hours of work and wages through international agreement.

Other bodies dealt with such matters as promotion of better health through international co-operation.

2 Aims. Members were bound by the Covenant to renounce war, respect treaties and obey international law. In case of dispute, members were to accept arbitration. They agreed on the need to reduce arms, and to control their manufacture.

These aims were to be put into effect through sanctions. All members agreed to use economic sanctions if necessary against any country branded unanimously as an aggressor by the League Council.

3 The League in action. Though handicapped by the absence of the USA and Russia as members, the League had some successes:

a Austria was given a loan to help her recovery.

b a dispute between Sweden and Finland over the ownership of the Aland Islands in the Baltic was settled by the League, who awarded them to Finland.

c however, the city of Vilna, which had been given to Lithuania by the Versailles Treaty, was seized by the Poles, and the League had to bow to this use of force.

d more serious was the Corfu incident in 1923. When some Italians were murdered on the Greek-Albanian frontier, Mussolini, Italy's new leader, ignored the League. The Italian Fleet bombarded and seized the island of Corfu from Greece. Only after the League had ordered Greece to pay compensation did Mussolini withdraw his forces.

e in 1926, border disputes between Greece and Turkey, and between Turkey and Iraq, were settled by League arbitration.

E The World Slump, 1929

1 This slump, which began in the USA (see Ch. 10) was the worst ever known. All over the world firms went bankrupt and unemployment rose. This was partly because the USA could no longer afford to buy from abroad, e.g. from Britain and Germany, and partly because Americans recalled the substantial loans they had made to countries such as Germany in the 1920s. Thus in Germany by 1932 there were six million out of work.

2 Attempts at international co-operation to overcome the slump, such as a World Economic Conference in London in 1933, were wrecked by the suspicions of individual countries. Each country had to fend for itself. This usually meant increasing tariffs to protect their own industries which, however, handicapped trade on a world-wide scale, and so made recovery even more difficult.

3 In general, the slump led to the rise of dictatorships (as in Germany) and strengthened existing ones (as in Italy). Such countries tended to use force as a means of getting out of their economic difficulties, by enabling them to capture new markets for their products.

4 One effect of the slump was the ending of reparations payments. In 1932 an agreement was reached at Lausanne by which Germany was to make one final payment of £150,000,000 in bonds. Soon afterwards Britain announced that she could not repay her loans to the USA and by 1934 all other countries had followed suit.

F Britain in the 1930s

Foreign affairs became increasingly important as the thirties wore on.

1 World peace was threatened by Japan, Italy and Germany in that order. Britain still considered herself a great power, in a sense the 'policeman of the world' whose duty it was to prevent wrongful aggression, whether by Japan in Manchuria, Italy in Abyssinia, or Germany in central Europe.

2 Yet in fact Britain was simply trying to do too much. Weakened by the effects of the First World War and the slump, without an effective

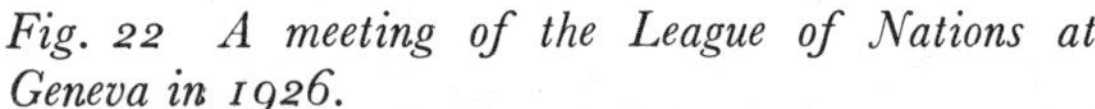

Fig. 22 A meeting of the League of Nations at Geneva in 1926.

ally, with armed forces the victims of the ten-year rule (especially the army), Britain was unable, though she did not see it at the time, to protect the rest of the world from the dictatorships.

In any case, there was widespread feeling in Britain in favour of pacifism and appeasement.

3 Pacifism, meaning a resolve not to fight under any circumstances, was strong in Britain in the 1930s.

A stream of books, e.g. Lloyd George's war memoirs and plays such as 'Journey's End' by R. C. Sheriff, showed the futility of the First World War, when stupid generals had lost hundreds of thousands of men in vain attacks, as at Verdun and the Somme. There was a feeling that the war had been a huge mistake, that, as Lloyd George put it, 'We all blundered into war'.

If there were no vast armaments, many believed, there simply could not be a war. Thus, in 1933, the Oxford Union (the debating society of Oxford University) passed a resolution that 'This House will not fight for King and Country'.

4 As the thirties wore on, and exaggerated reports of Germany's growing air power

Fig. 23 Girl snipers supporting the Spanish Government forces in Toledo, 1936, during the Civil War.

reached Britain, there was dread of air attack, strengthened by events in Spain, where the town of Guernica, for instance, was flattened by Franco's German bombers. In fact in 1939 the British Government believed that the first two months of war would see tremendous air attacks by Germany, causing almost two million civilian casualties in this country. As early as 1932 Baldwin had told the Commons that 'The bomber will always get through'.

5 Many people still believed, almost desperately, in the power of the League of Nations to prevent a war by means of sanctions against an aggressor. Thus when in 1934 the League organised a poll of all householders throughout Britain, the so-called peace ballot, over ten million out of eleven and a half replied in favour of international disarmament and 'collective security' as support for the League was called.

Support for the League was strong in the Labour and Liberal Parties. Until 1937 the Labour Party voted steadily in the Commons against rearmament. Yet many realised that some rearmament would be necessary if force were to be used by the League against an aggressor.

6 Against this background, appeasement, meaning securing peace by satisfying the real grievances of a dissatisfied country (usually Hitler's Germany), became the main feature of British foreign policy. There were several other reasons for this:

a many in Britain felt that Germany had been harshly treated at Versailles, and so deserved sympathetic treatment of her outstanding grievances. Each demand Hitler put forward was 'his last' according to him, and so in 1937–9 many British people felt that by giving in to him an unnecessary war could be avoided.

b at first, Hitler seemed to be doing 'a good job' in Germany at restoring order and bringing about an economic revival. After all, Britain needed a prosperous Germany as a customer.

c also, if Hitler did kill and imprison his opponents, such as the Communists, it was no worse than they had done to others. Many of the facts about his brutal treatment of the Jews were not printed by the British press, or not believed if they were. Many in Britain were still concerned about the threat of Communism spreading from Russia into Europe. Hitler's Germany seemed a good barrier against this.

d in 1938 over Czechoslovakia and in 1939 over Poland Britain realised that, even if she went to war with Germany, she was unable to help these countries in any practical way to resist German attack.

Britain had no effective ally. The USA was aloof from European affairs; Russia hoped to see Germany involved in a stalemate war with Britain and France; France was divided internally, with important groups supporting the dictators, and with her army equipped only for defence. Even the Dominions made it clear in 1937–8 that they favoured appeasement.

G The Far East

In the early 1930s the main threat to peace and security seemed to be not in Europe but the Japanese in the Far East.

1 Manchuria, 1931–2. Japan suffered severely from the world depression, and her army, which was almost independent of her government, determined to seize the Chinese province of Manchuria to open up a market for Japanese goods.

Manchuria belonged in theory to China, but was in fact usually in a state of lawlessness as the Chinese Government was so weak. Therefore, using as an excuse an explosion near the Japanese garrison at Mukden, on the South Manchurian Railway, Japanese troops seized Manchuria in September 1931. The following year, 1932, the Japanese made it into the puppet 'empire' of Manchukuo, under the Emperor Henry Pu-i.

China complained to the League of Nations accusing Japan of aggression, and the League, supported by Britain, set up a commission under Lord Lytton to investigate. In its report, the Lytton Commission condemned Japan for aggression. Japan then withdrew from the League, which took no further action, and in 1933 China recognised Manchukuo's independence.

2 The failure of Britain and the League to stop Japan has since been condemned by many historians, who see it as the first act of aggression in a chain that led up to the Second World War. Yet it must be remembered that:

a the Japanese claimed that they were merely restoring law and order in Manchuria, and other countries had done this before in China, e.g. Britain at Shanghai in 1927.

b Russia and the USA were not even members of the League, and the USA was keen to keep on good terms with Japan, a valued customer.

c Britain alone (of the League's members) had the sea power to act, but her fleet in the Far East was too weak to take on the Japanese single-handed. In any case, she was in the worst stage of the slump, and in no position to fight a major war.

3 China. In July 1937 China herself was attacked by Japan. This followed an incident at the Marco Polo Bridge (Peking) when Japanese troops were allegedly fired upon by Chinese. China appealed to the League again.

Fig. 24 Victorious Japanese troops entering a walled city in North China, 1937.

By this time the League was quite ineffective (see page 31). Britain was too concerned with affairs in Europe to be able to take on Japan. The USA refused to take any military action against Japan, though attitudes in the States were hardening against the aggressor.

4 Chinese resistance was weak, and by the time the Second World War spread to the Far East in 1941, Japan controlled most of the important cities and ports of eastern China. Only by retreating to western China (and moving the capital from Nanking to Chungking) could China's government and armies survive.

Yet Japan claimed she was only restoring the peace in China, not attacking, and referred to the matter as the 'China Incident'.

Fig. 25   German troops re-enter the Rhineland, 1936.

H Hitler, 1933–6

1 Hitler, who came to power in Germany in 1933 (see Ch. 5) had earlier stated his aims in foreign policy in his book, 'Mein Kampf':

a Germany must be strong, and a great power, so that she could gain territory ('Lebensraum' or 'living space') in the east of Europe, and take her place at the head of Europe in a new 'World Order'.

b to do this she must rearm, and build up her navy, army and air force.

c this meant that the 'Diktat' of Versailles must be renounced by Germany.

d Germany's colonies, lost at Versailles, must be restored to her, and the Communist threat in the east must be crushed.

e the various groups of Germans in eastern Europe, now under foreign rule in e.g. Poland and Czechoslovakia, must be reunited with the German fatherland.

2 German rearmament. A world Disarmament Conference had started to meet in 1932. When Hitler came to power, Germany walked out of this, and left the League of Nations in 1933.

Hitler reintroduced conscription for the armed forces, started to build up an air force (the Luftwaffe) and to equip his armies with the latest tanks. All this was in defiance of the Treaty of Versailles, as were his plans to build up the German Navy.

Hitler used as his excuse that general disarmament had been promised at Versailles, but that only Germany had been forced to do so. Many people in Britain thought that Germany had a case here. And Hitler was careful to give a peaceful impression, e.g. in 1934 he signed a ten-year non-aggression pact with Poland.

3 The Saar. Hitler's first success in foreign policy came in 1935, when the Saar, under French control for fifteen years since the Versailles Treaty, voted overwhelmingly to be reunited with Germany.

4 The Rhineland. The following year, 1936, German troops marched into the Rhineland, which was demilitarised under the Treaty of Versailles. Here Hitler took a great risk, for united action by France, Poland and the Czechs would have defeated Germany.

Yet the other countries were divided. The French Army was not trained or equipped to attack Germany, and Britain had hardly any troops to send. Poland and Czechoslovakia would not act unless France did, and France would do nothing without Britain. In Britain, the general opinion was that the Germans were only 'marching into their own backyard', and the government refused to act, especially as it was by now more concerned with events in Abyssinia.

Germany could now fortify her frontier with the west, and did so, building the 'Siegfried Line' of defences.

I Abyssinia

1 The successful Italian invasion of Abyssinia in 1935–6 showed the weakness of the League of Nations and marked the end of collective security through the League. From then on the League was of little importance in international affairs.

2 In the 1920s Italy had been friendly with Abyssinia, but in the early 1930s Mussolini, hoping for glory abroad to bolster his rule in Italy, and seeking to found a second Roman Empire in east Africa, decided on its conquest.

3 He used a border skirmish at Walwal in late 1934 as an excuse, and invaded in October 1935. By May 1936 Abyssinia had been conquered. Mussolini's army and air force, though in fact weak by European standards (as the Second World War was to show) easily defeated the Abyssinian Emperor Haile Selassie. Armed mostly with spears, the Abyssinian troops stood no chance against the guns, tanks and poison gas of the Italians.

4 The attack put Britain and France in a dilemma. Neither wished to see Italy strong in east Africa, and public feeling in both countries was strong against the aggressor. Yet the French Prime Minister, Laval, and the British Foreign Secretary, Sir Samuel Hoare, both feared to drive Mussolini into alliance with Hitler. Thus in April 1935, at Stresa, Britain, France and Italy had signed an agreement to maintain the Locarno Treaties.

The war was very popular in Italy, where the people looked forward to avenging Italy's defeat by Abyssinia at Adowa in 1896.

Also, Britain and France thought that Italy was much stronger than was really the case. Mussolini's boasts of mobilising 'eight million bayonets' and 'blotting out the sun with his aircraft' were taken seriously, and the British Navy doubted its ability to hold the Mediterranean against the Italian Fleet.

5 Thus Hoare and Laval agreed secretly in late 1935 that Abyssinia should be partitioned, giving most of it to Italy. News of this leaked out, however, and such was the public outcry in Britain that Baldwin's government had to reject the agreement, and Hoare was forced to resign as Foreign Secretary, Anthony Eden, later Lord Avon, taking his place.

6 The League imposed economic, but not military, sanctions. These did not include oil and coal, however, both vital to Italy, and in any case countries outside the League continued to supply her. The result was to annoy Mussolini but not to stop him.

7 Mussolini tore up the Stresa Agreement, and in late 1936 signed a treaty of co-operation with Hitler. In 1937 he signed the Anti-Comintern pact with Japan and Germany, aimed against Russia. Thus the Abyssinian affair had the very worst results for Britain and the League.

Fig. 26 The Führer and the Duce, 1937.

J Spain

Britain and France suffered a further diplomatic defeat in Spain.

1 In 1936 a 'popular front' government of Republicans, Socialists, Communists and Anarchists took office in Spain. They were opposed by the Falangists (Fascist nationalists), who included monarchists, industrialists and the army. The result was a rising, starting in Morocco, of Falangists led by General Franco, which spread quickly to the mainland of Spain.

2 The French Premier, Léon Blum, and many people in Britain were anxious to help the government forces, but Blum's Cabinet was divided, as was the British. Many in France and Britain did not want to help a régime that depended on Communist support.

Germany and Italy supported Franco. Hitler and Mussolini both wanted to see Spain ruled by a government friendly to them, and to stop the spread of Communism.

3 However in 1936 Britain, France, Germany and Italy signed a 'non-intervention' agreement, meaning that they would not interfere in Spain or help either side with arms or men. This was a farce. Britain and France kept to it, refusing to sell arms to the Spanish Government, but Germany and Italy ignored the agreement. Italy sent thousands of troops to help Franco, and Germany sent tanks and air force squadrons. Spain became a trying-out ground for Hitler's new forces, e.g. the Luftwaffe.

Fig. 27 Germans' triumphant entry into Vienna, 1938.

4 The Republican (government) forces received some help from Russia, and an International Brigade of volunteers from all over the world fought for a time on its side. The struggle in Spain was a terribly destructive one, with no mercy shown by either side, and it took Franco's forces until May 1939, when he captured Madrid, to gain control of the whole country.

5 Meanwhile, in Britain, Neville Chamberlain had succeeded Baldwin as Prime Minister, and was determined to reach a peaceful settlement in Europe. To do this, he still hoped for Mussolini's support against Hitler. Differences over how to achieve this led Eden to resign as Foreign Secretary. He was replaced by Halifax.

K Austria, 1938

1 Hitler felt strong enough by early 1938 to unite Austria and Germany (the 'Anschluss'). This was forbidden by the Treaty of Versailles, though the people of Austria were Germans by race and language. Hitler himself had been born there.

In February he told the Austrian Chancellor, von Schuschnigg, that a leading Austrian Nazi, Seyss-Inquart, must be made Minister of the Interior (with control of the police force) and that Austria must cooperate with Germany.

2 When von Schuschnigg proposed a plebiscite or popular vote in Austria on Germany's demands, Hitler feared the result would be against him, and so in March German forces crossed the border and took over Austria. The only country capable of stopping him was Italy, and Mussolini had promised not to interfere.

Plebiscites in Germany and Austria conducted by the Nazis, showed, of course, a great majority in favour of the Anschluss.

3 This was a big success for Germany. She now had a gateway to the Balkans, and surrounded much of Czechoslovakia on three sides, besides adding seven million more Germans to her numbers. Yet in Britain many felt that as the Austrians were Germans anyway, Britain should not intervene, and Hitler, of course, promised the Czechs that they had nothing to fear from Germany.

L Czechoslovakia, 1938–9

By May 1938, however, Hitler was telling his generals that he was determined 'to smash Czechoslovakia' in the near future.

1 On Hitler's orders, the Germans who lived in the Sudetenland (parts of Czechoslovakia bordering Germany) demanded that the area become part of the German Reich, and demonstrated violently against Czech 'oppression'. In his speeches on the matter, Hitler became increasingly violent in his attacks on the Czechs and their President, Beneš.

2 Britain's Premier, Chamberlain, intervened in September 1938, and flew to meet Hitler, the first of several meetings which led up to the Munich Agreement.

Hitler was in no mood to negotiate. He seems to have wanted not just the Sudetenland, but to obtain it by war on the Czechs.

After Chamberlain arrived back in Britain from his second meeting with Hitler, Britain issued a warning that she would fight if Germany attacked Czechoslovakia. Air-raid shelters were dug in London, and the fleet mobilised.

3 Now Hitler, persuaded partly by Mussolini, who knew that Italy was not ready for war, drew back, and agreed to a conference on the Czech problem in Munich. (In fact, Chamberlain believed that the Czechs would have to give in to Hitler's demands, as we had no means of helping them.)

At Munich in September 1938, Chamberlain, Daladier of France, Hitler and Mussolini signed an agreement giving Germany almost all she had asked. The Czechs were not even invited to the discussions, just told they would have to agree. The Sudetenland, which included many Czechs, was given to Germany. President Beneš resigned.

4 This was a great triumph for Hitler. Yet Chamberlain, who called Czechoslovakia 'a faraway country of which we know nothing', claimed on his return to London to have brought back 'peace in our time', and was wildly cheered when he did so. In Parliament, Winston Churchill was one of the few MPs who attacked the settlement. He warned that Hitler would soon want more. In fact Britain and her allies had differed on how to stop Hitler, as he knew

they would:

a Britain had few troops to send to fight Germany, and little modern equipment for them. The RAF was still weak (e.g. most fighter squadrons were still equipped with biplanes).

b the French Army expected a bloody defeat if launched into an attack on the Siegfried Line.

c the Dominions would not have supported Britain in a war over Czechoslovakia.

d Russia might have fought on the British side, but might (as happened in 1939) have been content to stand aside.

e Poland and Hungary were glad of the opportunity that Munich gave them to seize portions of Czech territory.

5 Hitler had the excuse at Munich that he was only demanding the return of Germans to the Fatherland (though in fact the Sudetenland had never been part of Germany). There was no such excuse when, in March 1939, he took over most of the rest of Czechoslovakia.

The Munich Agreement had meant the Czechs surrendering their mountain fortifications against Germany, thus leaving their country defenceless. So, when Slovaks and Ruthenes in Czechoslovakia demanded self-government, Hitler summoned Beneš' successor, President Hacha, to Berlin, and ordered him to

Fig. 28 Chamberlain just arrived back by air from Munich to a hero's welcome.

place Czechoslovakia under Germany's 'protection'. Hitler said Prague, the Czech capital, would be bombed to the ground if this was not done.

Thus the Czechs had to give in. Bohemia and Moravia became part of Germany, with Slovakia a German 'Protectorate'. The Hungarians took Ruthenia. (A few days later, Germany took Memel, on the Baltic, from Lithuania.)

6 These events had a great effect in Britain. Hitler's Germany was now seen to be bent on dominating Europe, if not the world. Chamberlain himself voiced these feelings in a speech at Birmingham, and the British Government joined with the French in offering a guarantee to Hitler's next most likely victim, Poland.

On Good Friday 1939, Mussolini, anxious not to be outshone by his ally Hitler, launched his armies into Albania, which quickly surrendered. Then, in May, he signed a treaty of alliance with Germany, the 'Pact of Steel'.

Fig. 29   The German-Russian agreement of 1939. Stalin and Ribbentrop (German Foreign Secretary) swallow what they have said in the past about each other's politics.

M Poland, 1939

1 It was clear to many in Britain, such as Churchill, that any guarantee to Poland was worthless without help from Russia. However, the Poles themselves would not have this, fearing Russia almost as much as they did Germany, and Chamberlain was not keen on the idea. Therefore negotiations between Britain and Russia in the summer of 1939 failed.

2 Instead, in August, Nazi Germany and Communist Russia signed a treaty of friendship, the secret parts of which agreed on a partition of Poland between the two countries. The 'friendship' part of the treaty was a sham. Both sides knew that war between Germany and Russia must come. However, it suited both parties for the time being.

If forced to fight Britain and France (something which he still hoped to avoid) Hitler would not, unlike Germany in 1914, have to fight Russia as well.

Stalin, the Russian leader, made a very serious mistake. He hoped that Germany would exhaust herself in a struggle with Britain and France. Instead, in 1940, she easily defeated France, and turned the might of her armies against Russia the following year.

3 However, Britain and France made it clear that their guarantees to Poland still held, and on 25 August, Britain signed a definite treaty of mutual assistance with Poland. Hitler, however, felt that the 'Men of Munich' were only bluffing, and would not fight, so ordered his armies to attack Poland on 1 September 1939.

Here Hitler made a mistake, for on 3 September, after Germany had ignored British demands to withdraw from Poland, Britain and France declared war on Germany.

N Britain's Preparations for War

1 Rearmament. As late as the general election of 1935 Baldwin had had to promise 'no great armaments'. His successor Chamberlain was distressed at having to spend millions of pounds on arms, which could have been used to improve living conditions and build schools, hospitals, etc. Yet in the late 1930s the threat from Germany was so clear that government and public opinion accepted the need for rearmament. Indeed, it was often forgotten later that many of the weapons which helped us first to defy, then to defeat Germany, originated in the plans drawn up by Chamberlain and his Ministers:

a the navy had fared better than the other two services between the wars and was a powerful force in September 1939. Many of the battleships were old, but new types of ships, such as the aircraft carrier, had been developed since 1918. A big programme of building anti-submarine and convoy escort vessels was under way when war broke out.

b the RAF underwent a big expansion programme in the late 1930s. New types of aircraft such as the eight-gun fighter (the Hurricane and Spitfire) and the four-engined bomber· were designed, though only the fighters were in service when war broke out. New factories were built to produce them. A vital development was the building of radar stations, based on an idea by Robert Watson-Watt, around the coast, to give warning of the approach of enemy aircraft, their speed, direction, height, and approximate numbers.

c as defence was of first importance, the Royal Navy and the RAF took priority in rearmament over the army. Thus when war broke out, the British Army was small and badly-equipped. Although Britain had pioneered the use of tanks, her army lagged far behind the Germans in both numbers of tanks and ideas on how best to use them. Conscription (for six months only) was introduced in 1939, for the first time in peacetime Britain.

2 Domestic preparations. The two main dangers were thought to be from food shortage and air attack:

a this time the government did not wait (as it had done in the First World War) until Britain faced starvation before acting to increase food output. Even before the war broke out, it called on farmers to plough up more land. This was so that more arable crops such as wheat, barley and potatoes could be grown. Farmers were offered cash to plough up grassland. The government built up a stockpile of tractors for use in wartime.

In addition, plans were made for food rationing, and, partly to help this to be put into effect, everybody in the United Kingdom was given a National Registration Number and an Identity Card.

b a full-scale programme of 'Air Raid Precautions' (ARP) was launched. Shelters were dug, and the 'blackout' was prepared. All windows were to be fitted with light-proof curtains or shutters, so as to give no guidance to enemy aircraft attacking at night. Street lamps were to be switched off and car headlamps dimmed. A force of full- and part-time Air Raid Wardens was recruited to help the rest of the civilian population in an air raid, and trained to tackle small fires, in first-aid and in rescue work. Air raid sirens were installed to give warning of air raids, and special warnings of gas attack laid down. All the population were issued with gas masks. A programme to evacuate children from towns into country districts was drawn up. Underlying all this was the fear of massive air attack when war started.

Fig. 30 Central Europe, 1935-9, showing the growth of Germany under Hitler.

A Origins of Mussolini's Dictatorship

1 Benito Mussolini was born in 1883. An outstanding speaker, he became a Socialist, and editor of that party's paper, 'Avanti!' At first he opposed Italy's entry into the war in 1914, but soon changed his opinion, probably having been bribed by the French, and said that Italy must join the Allies. Expelled from the Socialist Party, he founded his own paper, 'Il Popolo d'Italia'. After serving in the army, where he was wounded, he returned to civilian life and founded the Fascist Party in 1919.

2 There was much violence in Italy at that time, and the Fascists or 'blackshirts' formed 'squads', paid by industrialists and landowners, to break strikes by force. Strikers and Socialist politicians were beaten up and made to swallow huge doses of castor oil. Some were shot. Their offices were wrecked, and their newspapers forced to close. Many demobilised and unemployed officers and men, with a taste for action and a desire to regain lost prestige, eagerly joined the squads.

3 Within a few years Mussolini was to become dictator of Italy, though in the elections of 1921 the Fascists gained only 35 seats.

Fig. 31 Following the 'March on Rome' of October 1922, Mussolini parades triumphantly.

B Reasons for Mussolini's Rise to Power

1 Background. Italy had become a unified state in 1871, yet serious problems remained:

a Italy was economically poor, with few raw materials and many areas of poor soil.

b the south especially was backward, and tended to fall behind the north.

c the parliamentary system had failed to bring Italy stable government. Ministries kept office only by bribery in the Chamber (Italian Parliament).

2 The situation in 1918–22. Rapid inflation led to rising prices, bread riots, strikes in towns and riots of peasants in the country:

a industry was hit by the ending of the war. Unemployment was made worse by the limiting of immigration by the USA.

b in the economic crisis of 1920–2, which led up to a general strike, factories were seized by workers, and industrialists were glad to use the Fascist squads to break the power of the trade unions and the Socialist Party.

c inspired by events in Russia, many peasants seized land and went on rent strike. Landowners employed Fascists to stop this.

d Italy as a whole was bitterly disappointed by the terms of the Treaty of Versailles, which gave Italy less than she had been promised by the Allies during the war.

e the middle classes and the Church feared a Communist revolution in Italy, and many came to see Mussolini as the strong man needed to stop this.

f the local police and prefects often helped the Fascists, or at least turned a blind eye to their activities.

3 The 'March on Rome', 28 October 1922. After his squads had broken the general strike of 1922, Mussolini organised the famous 'March on Rome'. 30 000 Fascists from all over Italy moved on Rome (though Mussolini himself stayed safely in Milan) and demanded that a new government be formed, with a majority of Fascist ministers.

The army and police could easily have crushed the Fascists, but, in a crucial decision, King Victor Emmanuel III refused to sign a decree imposing martial law. Instead, he sent for Mussolini (who arrived in Rome by train) and asked him to form a government.

C Mussolini in Power

1 Government and Parliament:

a at first many Liberals supported Mussolini, and only gradually did Italians realise what they had let themselves in for.

b by the electoral law of 1923 the party gaining most votes in a general election was to be given two-thirds of the seats in the Chamber. This the Fascists did in the 1924 election, and so had a stable majority.

In the same year, Mussolini made the Fascist Grand Council (made up of the leaders of Fascism) into a rival of the Cabinet. (In 1929 the Fascist Grand Council replaced the Cabinet.)

c his weakest moment was in 1924, when the Socialist leader Matteotti was murdered by Fascists. This caused a wave of anger in Italy, and the opposition parties withdrew from the Chamber in protest. Yet once again the King gave Mussolini vital support, and this encouraged the latter to declare himself dictator the following year.

d government was centralised in Mussolini's hands. Apart from being Prime Minister, he was at one time his own Minister of the Interior, Foreign Secretary, and head of the army, navy and air force as well!

Once in power, he abolished all other parties, and at elections the Italian people were reduced to voting 'yes' or 'no' for a list of Fascist candidates (by the electoral law of 1928).

In 1939 Mussolini abolished Parliament and replaced it with a 'Council of Corporations and Fasces' (see page 38).

2 The strengthening of Mussolini's position:

a the police were purged of all opposition elements, and a secret police (OVRA) was formed to deal ruthlessly with all open or secret resistance to the régime.

b in the early years of his rule, opponents such as Communists and Socialists were beaten up or made to drink castor oil if their offences were minor. More serious opposition was dealt with by imprisonment or assassination. Even exiles were not safe. By about 1925 open opposition in Italy had become rare.

c a new and strict penal code was introduced, much of which is still in force. Judges were all reliable Fascists. Trial by jury was abolished, and special tribunals dealt with political offenders. Ordinary crime decreased, and the power of the Mafia secret society was crippled for a time.

d education, from infant to university levels, was strictly controlled to brainwash the young with Fascist ideas, and build up the myth of Mussolini as a superman. Fascist youth organisations, e.g. the Balilla, catered for boys and girls of all ages.

e the press was made to serve the state. Opposition newspapers were all closed down or taken over.

Fig. 32 The Duce addresses his people. Mussolini was a brilliant orator, and master of propaganda tricks, e.g. he insisted that photographs of him should be taken from a low level, so he would look taller than he in fact was.

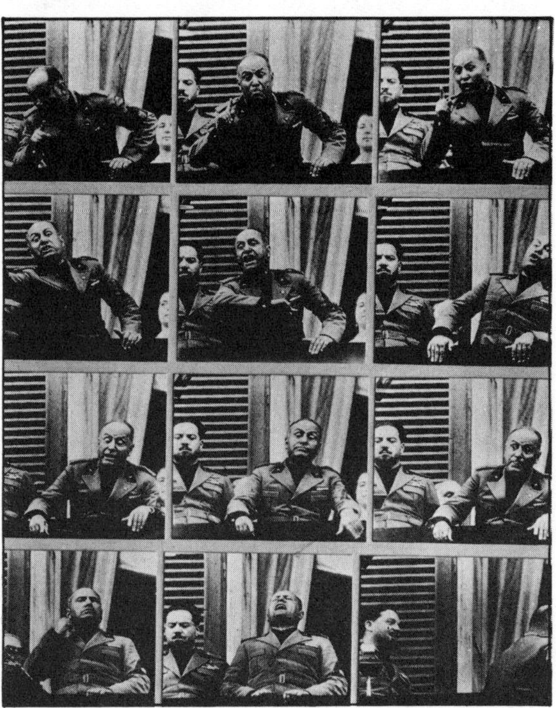

f possibly Mussolini's greatest triumph in his domestic policies was the Concordat of 1929, which healed the breach between Church and State which had existed in Italy since unification.

The Pope became ruler of the tiny Vatican City in Rome, while Mussolini agreed to pay the Papacy compensation in cash and in government bonds for lands and property lost by the Church in 1870. Catholicism was to become the official religion of the State.

Yet Mussolini was to come into increasing conflict with the Church over such matters as instruction in schools, and the rival claims of Catholic and Fascist youth organisations.

g strikes were forbidden, and trade unions disbanded. Their place was taken by 'Corporations' of employers and workers, one for each group of industries. The professions, e.g. the law, were also represented. The Corporations were supposed to work with the government in running various industries, and in 1939 replaced the Chamber, yet in fact seem to have achieved little, although there was a large bureaucracy to run them.

h both in domestic and foreign affairs Mussolini proved himself an 'artist in propaganda'. He was built up as a superman who knew all and who worked tirelessly for the Italian people. 'Mussolini is always Right', 'Believe, Obey, Fight', were typical Fascist slogans. He took the title of 'Duce' ('Leader' – once used by the great Italian patriot Garibaldi). He made great use of mass rallies of his 'blackshirts' and demonstrations.

3 Domestic policies:

a he failed to solve any of Italy's main problems, apart from bringing her a period of freedom from internal strife. Most Italians came to accept his rule, yet beneath the façade of businesslike activity there was much corruption and idleness in Fascist Italy.

b programmes of irrigation, drainage and afforestation were undertaken. His greatest achievement here was to drain the Pontine marshes near Rome.

c convinced that Italy needed to increase her population if she were to be a great power, he started an unsuccessful campaign (the 'Battle for Births') to increase the Italian birth-rate, by such means as tax incentives for large families.

d aiming to make Italy self-sufficient in wheat he launched the 'Battle for Grain' with more success. Yet much of the land converted to wheat-growing was better suited to other crops, and imported wheat would have been cheaper.

e a large programme of public buildings and works was started, partly to relieve unemployment, partly to build up Mussolini's reputation. One example was the building of the 'autostrade' roads.

f he 'made the trains run on time', partly by threats to conscript late-running drivers into the army.

g industry was encouraged by state subsidies and a protectionist tariff policy, yet no great growth took place, and prices were high.

h he tried to persuade Italians and others that his Italy was the successor to the Roman Empire of old. The Fasces itself (the Fascist emblem) was an old Roman symbol of authority. Mussolini reintroduced the Roman salute, and tried to bring in a new calendar with Roman numerals, dating from the March on Rome. Thus 1936 became 'Anno XIV.'

Fig. 33 Mussolini made a great show of lending a hand himself, as here during the corn harvest.

i only later in his rule did Mussolini start to imitate Hitler and introduce anti-Jewish laws, and then nothing like so severely as in Germany. Jews were dismissed from the forces and government jobs, but Italy saw nothing to compare with the horrors of Hitler's 'Final Solution' (see Ch. 5).

j Italy scored some spectacular victories in car and aircraft racing, but these machines were produced on a very limited scale, and were not robust enough for warfare.

4 Assessment of Mussolini:

a many people at the time were taken in, for a while at any rate, by Mussolini's supposed success in domestic policy, including Churchill and Lloyd George. Yet the most that can be said for him is that he ended civil war and brought stability for a while, but at a high price in lost freedom.

b in economic matters Fascism's performance was dismal:

The budget often failed to balance, especially as a result of Mussolini's adventures in Spain and Abyssinia, which caused an increase in income tax.

There was a chronic trade deficit as exports fell.

Industrial workers and civil servants suffered reductions in wages, and had to work longer hours in many cases, e.g. the eight-hour day was abolished.

D Foreign Policies

(See Ch. 3 for further details.)

1 Fascist ideology taught that:

a Italy must be a strong and powerful force to be reckoned with among the great powers, and must build up a colonial empire.

b war was the destiny of man, where he showed to the best advantage.

Thus Mussolini tried to follow a vigorous foreign policy, especially in the later 1930s, when he tried to copy Hitler.

2 Yet Italy was not strong enough industrially. Long before, Bismarck had called her a country with 'a big mouth but poor teeth'.

He built up the Italian Navy, yet when war came it proved unable to defend Italy's long coastline, and lack of fuel handicapped training.

In 1940 Italy had a fair-sized air force, but most of the machines were out of date.

The army was large in numbers, but poorly equipped.

3 Soon after taking power, Mussolini showed the kind of foreign policy he favoured by his bombardment of Corfu, in 1923.

4 In the early 1930s he was at first suspicious of Hitler, but largely as a result of the Abyssinian war he became Hitler's ally.

5 The Abyssinian campaign was very popular in Italy, and greatly increased Mussolini's prestige there. Yet it brought Italy no real gain, (nor did her intervention in Spain on Franco's side), and Abyssinia was lost in 1941.

6 To match Hitler's occupation of Czechoslovakia in 1939, Mussolini seized Albania. Then, in 1940, with France about to collapse, he grabbed the 'chance of a thousand years' to enter the war on Germany's side in the hope of easy pickings.

E Mussolini's Fall

1 By 1943 Italy faced a nightmare situation:

a she had been defeated by the Allies in Africa, and had lost her Empire there.

b she now faced heavy air attack and invasion by the Allied forces.

c there were grave shortages of food and raw materials.

d the Italian attack on Greece in late 1940 had failed, and Germany had had to come to Italy's rescue.

e the Italian Fleet suffered defeat at Taranto (November 1940) and Cape Matapan (March 1941).

2 Following the Allied landings in Sicily in July 1943, with invasion of Italy imminent, the Fascist Grand Council met and a motion highly critical of Mussolini was passed (24 July 1943).

The King had him arrested the next day, and Italy had made peace with the Allies by September. Mussolini was imprisoned, but rescued by German paratroops.

3 He then set up the puppet Republic of Salo in northern Italy, which was still held by the Germans. In April 1945, with the collapse of German resistance in Italy, he tried to escape to Switzerland. He was caught by Communist partisans and shot.

A Hitler to 1933

1 Adolf Hitler, the son of a customs official, was born in Austria in 1889. He lived in Vienna as a young man, and had a succession of humble jobs, such as a sign-writer. On the outbreak of war in 1914 he joined the German Army and became a corporal. He was decorated with the Iron Cross for bravery.

After the war he joined the German Workers' Party, which he renamed the National Socialist (Nazi) Party. It had only a handful of members, and Hitler soon became its President. He showed hypnotic powers as an orator, though most people in the early twenties dismissed him as a harmless crank. Yet within just over ten years he was dictator of Germany.

The rise of dictatorships took place all over Europe, in the troubled years between the wars. As parliamentary and democratic rule failed to solve the difficulties facing governments, especially after the slump of 1929, countries such as Germany, Austria, Poland and others placed power in the hands of one man, who became an absolute ruler. Typically, Parliaments and opposition parties were abolished, as were trade unions. The dictator was built up by a powerful propaganda machine into a sort of father figure,

who would solve all his country's problems, if the people gave him unquestioning obedience. This is what had happened in Italy.

To understand Hitler's rise to power, we must understand the background of events and feelings in Germany.

2 After the revolution of 1918 in Germany, which led to the abdication of the Kaiser and the end of the Monarchy, Germany became a republic with a democratic Constitution, the Weimar Republic, named after the town where its national assembly first met. From the first this was unstable:

a the Republic had no deep roots in Germany, nor had the idea of democracy. Also, it was tainted as something imposed by the victorious Allies, and as having accepted the Treaty of Versailles.

b the lack of an Emperor left a gap which was not easily filled on the German political scene.

c the political parties were immature, and governments tended to be weak, as for years the Communists refused to work with any other party, and the Catholic Centre Party refused to co-operate with the Socialists.

d the Versailles Settlement was widely hated in Germany because:

The war guilt clause blamed Germany.

Germany was saddled with a heavy burden of reparations, and lost all of her colonies and some of her own territory in Europe.

3 Thus, the idea put forward by Hitler that Germany had been betrayed in 1918 by a 'stab in the back' was accepted, as was his story that 'traitors' such as Jews, pacifists and Communists had been responsible.

Yet, after a shaky start, when it had barely managed to survive the Spartacist plot by Communists and the Kapp Putsch (an attempt by right-wing Monarchists to overthrow the government), the Weimar Republic survived the runaway inflation of 1923.

In November of that year, Hitler attempted to seize power by force in an armed rising or 'putsch' in Munich. This was a flop. He was arrested and sentenced to five years imprisonment. Actually, he was released the following year, but had used the time in Landsberg prison

Fig. 34 Hitler speaking. He was a brilliant orator, and had an almost hypnotic hold over his audiences.

to express his ideas in a famous book, 'Mein Kampf' (My Struggle):

a the Germans, he wrote, were the Aryan 'master race' or 'Herrenvolk'. They needed 'living space' (Lebensraum) which would be found in the east at the expense of the Poles, Slavs and Russians. All these races, indeed all other races, were inferior to the 'master race'. Lowest of all came the Jewish 'Untermenschen' or 'subhumans'.

b as far as Hitler was concerned, the individual existed only to serve the state, which had an absolute right to everybody's property and life.

c Germany herself must be strong, economically and militarily, so that she could overthrow the hated 'Diktat' of Versailles.

d among nations, as among wild animals, 'survival of the fittest' was the rule.

4 Germany seemed to be recovering well from the war in the years 1924–9, thanks mainly to short-term loans from America. This prosperity ended in the Wall Street crash of 1929, which started the world slump. American loans were recalled, world trade fell, and so did wages and prices.

In Germany factory after factory closed down until in 1931 there were nearly 6 000 000 unemployed. Thus the Nazis, who had gained only 12 Reichstag seats in 1928, soon became the biggest party there.

5 By 1932 Hitler was attracting widespread support in Germany:

a there was a strong current of nationalism in Germany, e.g. in the universities and civil service, to which Hitler made a great appeal.

b the army were interested in his promises of rearmament, as were Germany's industrialists.

c the middle classes were embittered by the inflation of 1923, when many had lost their savings, and now looked for a 'strong man' to prevent a repetition.

d the wealthy thought Hitler would protect them from the Communists and Socialists.

e many Germans of all classes thought he would make Germany strong enough to resist the Bolshevik threat from the east.

f Hitler particularly appealed to the young as a man of ideals and action. (The average age of Nazi Reichstag members was much lower than in other parties.)

g ex-servicemen found they could recover some of the prestige and dignity they had had during the war when wearing a Nazi uniform.

h many people, e.g. in the churches, thought Hitler was a sincere and honest man who would 'clean up' German politics.

i Hitler, helped by the talents of Goebbels, made the most of this wide appeal through his powers as an orator, and his mastery of propaganda.

B Hitler Takes Power in 1933

1 By this time there was widespread violence in Germany, with political murders and street fights between Nazis and Communists an everyday event.

Hitler relied on his SA, the brownshirts (Sturmabteilung or stormtroopers), led by Ernst Röhm. These, numbering 400 000, showed the Nazis' power by their parades and demonstrations, and broke up opponents' meetings, beat them up, and generally caused trouble.

2 in the July 1932 elections, the Nazis gained 230 seats in the Reichstag (though still well short of a majority), and Hitler ran, unsuccessfully, as a Presidential candidate. Hindenburg was elected again.

Following another general election and a succession of short-lived governments, Hindenburg appointed Hitler Chancellor on 30 January 1933. In the new Cabinet, Nazis were in a minority, but Hitler seized this chance to demand yet another general election.

3 Amid increasing violence, tension reached a new peak when the Reichstag building in Berlin was destroyed by fire. A Dutch Communist, van der Lubbe, was responsible. Although he had acted alone, the Nazis said the fire was part of a Communist plot to take over Germany, and Hitler persuaded Hindenburg to suspend the guarantees of freedom of speech and of the press, and of personal liberty, which were written into the Constitution.

Goering (one of Hitler's closest followers and head of the Prussian police) and Frick (the Nazi Minister of the Interior), enrolled thousands of stormtroopers into the police. This meant that the Nazi thugs could attack their opponents without any restraint.

4 Even so, the Nazi Party received only 44% of the votes in the general election of March 1933, and with their Nationalist allies commanded a tiny majority in the Reichstag, not the two-thirds majority needed to amend the Constitution. However, the Communist deputies were all arrested or in hiding, as were some of the Socialists. The other non-Nazi parties, in desperation, voted by 441 votes to 94 for the Nazi Enabling Act which gave the Chancellor, Hitler, power to rule by decree for four years without summoning the Reichstag.

5 Hitler now went on to crush all opposition:

a all parties except the Nazis were banned, as were the trade unions. All workers had to join the Nazi 'German Labour Front'.

b the press was silenced, and became a vehicle for Nazi propaganda.

c in the churches, priests and ministers who attacked the Nazis, such as the Catholic Cardinal Faulhaber and the Protestant Pastor Niemoeller, were ignored or arrested. Yet many in the churches hesitated to oppose Hitler at first until the evil nature of his rule became clear. By then it was too late to do anything.

For instance, in 1933 Hitler signed a Concordat (agreement on Church matters) with the Vatican, which he soon ignored.

Thus Catholic youth movements were dissolved and all children and young people were forced to join Nazi movements such as the Hitler Youth and Hitler Maidens, where they received teaching which was against Christianity.

d the dreaded Gestapo, or secret state police, proved effective in dealing with any opponents of the régime, whether open or secret. The Gestapo was a branch of the SS (Schutzstaffeln or Protection Squads) the organisation which rivalled and then crushed the SA.

The law courts were purged of any non-Nazis. Judges, for instance, had to support the government.

A new and drastic penal code was introduced and the number of executions rose. Undesir-ables who were not executed were sent to one of the dreaded concentration camps.

e the German State was more highly centralised than ever before or since. The rights of the local states or Lander were abolished, and they were ruled by Gauleiters (Nazi officials).

f on the death of Hindenburg in August 1934, Hitler became President as well as Chancellor, though he was in fact called Führer (leader). Meanwhile, in June, he had dealt with opposition in his own party.

g Ernst Röhm had hoped that his SA would increase in power, but Germany's Army leaders, whose support Hitler needed, feared this rivalry. Also, German industrialists were afraid that the Nazi Government might carry out a radical Socialist policy, as some of its supporters wished.

Therefore, to win the support of the army and industrialists, Hitler purged his followers in the 'Night of the Long Knives' on 30 June. Several hundreds of his colleagues, and others who had offended him in some way, were murdered, prominent among them being Röhm.

The SA now took a back seat in Nazi affairs, and the SS, headed by Heinrich Himmler, became the leading Nazi uniformed organisation.

h once he felt strong enough, Hitler purged the army High Command. On becoming President, he ordered all officers and men to swear an oath of allegiance to him personally. This was something very important to most German soldiers. Then in 1938 he dismissed the War Minister and the Commander-in-Chief of the army, and became head of all the armed forces himself.

i Hitler gave the name 'Gleichschaltung' (co-ordination) to the Nazi domination of every aspect of German political, social, economic and cultural life. To the 'New Germany' he gave the name 'Third Reich' and boasted it would last for a thousand years.

C Hitler Builds up Germany's Strength

1 Hitler solved the unemployment problem by:

42

a conscripting many men for the forces.

b creating many jobs in factories by his re-armament programme.

c creating jobs in public works, e.g. building the 'Autobahnen' or motorways, and af-forestation programmes.

d the full-time enrolling of many of his supporters in Nazi organisations.

e encouraging women to give up work, especially in the professions. Hitler was a firm believer that 'woman's place is in the home'.

2 His general economic programme was one of 'Autarky' i.e. making Germany self-sufficient. To this end much research was carried out into artificial products, such as synthetic rubber and oil.

Hitler's great projects were paid for by higher taxes and prices. As wages remained fairly static, and prices rose, the workers' standard of living fell. However, there were no longer any trade unions to protest about this.

Also, Hitler borrowed much money inside Germany, sometimes compulsorily.

3 Germany's armed forces grew rapidly:

a the army's strength was built up through conscription, and it was equipped with the latest weapons, e.g. tanks.

b an air force or 'Luftwaffe' was created under the leadership of Goering.

c the navy was built up, but not as quickly as the other two services.

D How Hitler Kept his Position

1 The German people were subjected to a barrage of Nazi propaganda from which it was difficult to escape, in the press, on radio, and in the cinema.

This was organised by the twisted genius of Goebbels. Hitler was fortunate that radio broadcasting and the talking picture had both been developed when he came to power.

2 His power as an orator was exploited to the full at mass rallies. The Nazis made much use of torchlight processions and marching songs.

3 The arts in general were made to serve Nazi aims, e.g. music, painting, architecture, literature and the theatre all had to correspond with standards laid down by the Nazi Party. Thus

Fig. 35   Hitler Youth at a Nazi Party rally.

Fig. 36   Nazi mass rally, Nuremberg, 1933.

Goebbels was both Minister of Propaganda and of Culture.

4 Education at all ages was strictly controlled:
a textbooks were written by Nazis, and teachers (who all had to be members of the National Socialist Teachers' League) had to put over the Party's message.
b higher education was discouraged, except where it trained someone to be of greater use to the State, and numbers at universities fell.
c from early childhood to old age there were a whole range of movements designed to brainwash their members into believing Nazi views, e.g. the Hitler Youth. Non-Nazi movements, such as the Boy Scouts, were banned.

5 Hitler had an almost mystical appeal to women, and his friendship with Eva Braun was kept strictly secret. His views on women seem old-fashioned to us today. He thought a woman's place was in the home, where she would raise a large family to provide future cannon-fodder for the Reich.

6 He was very successful in stirring up anti-semitism. This diverted the German people's attention away from their troubles:
a by the Nuremberg Laws of 1935 Jews (defined as all who had one or more Jewish grandparents) lost all rights as citizens, and were banned from the professions, e.g. medicine and the law. Intermarriage between Jews and non-Jews was forbidden.
b in November 1938 the Nazis used the assassination of a German diplomat by a young Jew in Paris as an excuse for an orgy of anti-semitism, beginning with the infamous 'Kristallnacht' (Crystal Night, or night of broken glass). Organised attacks, backed by the police, took place on Jewish businesses and synagogues, while many Jews were beaten up or flogged in the streets. In addition, the government imposed an enormous fine on the Jewish community as a whole.
c Jews were encouraged to leave Germany, but had to leave all their property behind. Those unable to leave were forced to wear the Star of David on their clothing, to sit apart from Aryans in public places and on public transport, and were made to perform humiliating tasks in public, such as scrubbing pavements. They had to live in special ghettoes.
d later, all Jews were rounded up and sent to concentration camps or death camps.

Yet anti-semitism cost Hitler dearly in the long run. Many talented Jews fled from Nazi persecution and then served the Allies during

Fig. 37 Front page of the Nazi anti-Jewish paper, 'Der Stürmer', edited by the notorious 'Jew-baiter' Julius Streicher. Such propaganda led to brutal ill-treatment for Jews unfortunate enough to live in Germany or German-occupied countries. Hitler's 'final solution' to the 'Jewish problem' meant that about six million Jews were rounded up by Gestapo squads and executed, many of them in 'extermination camps' like Auschwitz. These were purpose-built with large gas chambers where victims could be executed hundreds at a time, and ovens where their remains were burnt.

the Second World War (e.g. Einstein and other pioneers of the atomic bomb).

Also, his treatment of Jews turned public opinion against him in countries such as Britain and the USA.

E Hitler's Germany in Wartime

1 At first, the war was popular in Germany:

a food rationing was introduced in 1939, but was not severe at first (as it later became).

b there was little effective bombing of Germany until 1942. Losses among the armed forces in the same period were light.

c the war was successful, and seemed to support Hitler's theory of the 'Blitzkrieg' or lightning war.

d in fact, not until 1942 were Germany's resources effectively mobilised for war production, helped by the recruitment of millions of slave labourers from all over Europe.

2 In 1942 the situation changed dramatically:

a on land and in the air Germany was on the retreat by the end of the year.

b in 1942 Allied bombing became almost non-stop, and much more accurate than before.

c yet the German people usually stood up well to this ordeal. There were tens of thousands of Gestapo agents and others listening and watching, ready to betray or arrest anyone who seemed in the least faint-hearted about the war. Any such waverers would be sentenced to death or a concentration camp, as would anyone found listening to the Allied radio.

d Goebbels (Hitler hardly appeared in public after 1942) by his speeches and tours of bombed areas persuaded the mass of the German people that they must stick it out until fearsome new V-weapons (secret vengeance weapons e.g. rocket bombs) had been developed, or the Allies disagreed among themselves.

e the nearest Hitler came to assassination was in the bomb plot of 20 July 1944 (see Ch. 6). Its failure meant another year of war, which ended soon after Hitler's suicide in 1945.

Fig. 38 New arrivals in a concentration camp. Here were sent any opponents of Nazism and many Jews, also habitual criminals and pacifists. Before and during the war hundreds of thousands were thus treated, and few came out alive. Food was so meagre that many starved, or died from infectious diseases like typhus. Some even resorted to cannibalism. Clothing and blankets were thin and huts unheated, so many died from exposure in winter. The SS guards inflicted brutal tortures and beatings which drove many inmates to suicide. Others died as a result of being used as human guinea-pigs in 'scientific experiments' such as exposure to extremely low air pressure.

Fig. 39 Wreckage after the bomb plot on Hitler's life, 20 July 1944.

A 1939

1 Poland. The Germans destroyed most of the Polish Air Force on the ground in the first hours of the war (1 September). Then the Nazi bombers, e.g. Stuka dive-bombers, could range at will over Poland's cities and country-side, bombing defenceless towns and machine-gunning refugee columns, setting a pattern that was to be repeated all over Europe.

The Polish Army put up a brave but hopeless fight. Its excellent cavalry was no use against the German 'panzers' (strong forces of tanks, supported by infantry in lorries and motorised artillery). On 17 September the Russians attacked Poland from the east, and by the 27th the last Polish resistance had ceased. Britain and France had been unable to help her in any way.

2 In the west, there was no attack by either side. The French stayed behind their 'Maginot Line' (a line of strong defences along their German frontier) and the tiny British Expeditionary Force (BEF) joined them. The Germans, of course, were busy in Poland. Thus few shots were fired on the Western Front, much to the amazement of many foreign countries, who called this the 'Phoney War'.

Britain and France had feared massive air attack, but this did not come until the following year. Actually, Hitler, as well as many people in France and some in Britain, still hoped for a peaceful settlement in the west.

3 At sea, the German surface fleet was too weak to challenge the Allied navies. As in the First World War, Germany hoped to hinder food supplies from abroad by the use of surface raiders and submarines, but in 1939 she had nothing like the number of submarines needed. One of them, however, in a daring attack, sank the battleship 'Royal Oak' in harbour at Scapa Flow. In December, the German pocket battleship 'Graf Spee' was driven into Monte-video harbour (Uruguay), at the battle of the River Plate, and later scuttled herself.

4 Other countries:

a in the USA President Roosevelt sympathised with the Allied cause, and came to believe that America must fight on the Allies' side. However, in the USA there was a strong body of isolationist opinion, people who believed that America should never have become involved in the First World War, and must at all costs stay out of the second one. Thus, Roosevelt found it very difficult to help the Allies in any way, particularly as he was up for re-election in late 1940.

b Russia, under Stalin, was building up her forces for the war she knew must come with Nazi Germany. She tried to improve her defences by setting up bases in the small Baltic states of Estonia, Latvia and Lithuania. When Finland refused to agree to similar demands, Russian armies attacked her in November. The Red Army did badly against a skilful Finnish defence, but sheer weight of numbers forced the Finns to agree to Russia's wishes in March 1940.

c Italy was too weak at that time to join in on Germany's side, and Mussolini decided to play a waiting game.

B 1940

This year was one of severe defeat for the Allies, and ended with most of western Europe under Hitler's control. Hitler's aims in the war at this stage were to reach a settlement in the west so that he could turn his forces against Russia, and so end the war quickly. He wanted a series of 'Blitzkrieg' or lightning wars, rather than a long

Fig. 40   German panzers.

drawn-out struggle.

1 Norway and Denmark. On 9 April, German troops occupied Denmark in less than a day, and other forces were landed, by sea and air, in Norway, which was important to Germany for the supply of iron ore from northern Sweden. The Germans were supported by a few Norwegians led by Vikdun Quisling, who gave his name to those who supported the Germans in other countries.

Britain and France sent forces to Norway to help the growing Norwegian resistance, but the poorly led and badly equipped expedition was forced to withdraw in a few weeks, and by 10 June, Norway was in Germany's hands.

2 Growing criticism of Chamberlain's leadership as Prime Minister came to a head in Parliament in early May, and in a critical vote a large number of Conservative MPs joined the Labour and Liberal opposition to him. This led to Chamberlain's resignation, and Winston Churchill replaced him as Prime Minister at the head of a Coalition Government on 10 May.

Churchill proved a great war leader. He put across to all British people his utter determination to win 'victory at all costs'. Where Chamberlain had dithered (Bomber Command spent the first six months of the war dropping propaganda leaflets on Germany), Churchill acted without hesitation (as he showed by the attack on the French Fleet at Oran in July – see page 49). A brilliant orator, his radio broadcasts inspired the 'man in the street'. He 'mobilised the English language and sent it into battle'.

3 Blitzkrieg in the west:

a Churchill took office on the day the Germans launched their main attack in the west. This offensive was planned by Hitler himself and confirmed his belief in himself as a military genius.

First, the Germans occupied Luxembourg and invaded Holland and Belgium. Holland surrendered in four days, but not in time to prevent a devastating German air attack on Rotterdam. Allied forces, including the BEF, advanced into Belgium, but the Belgian Army was ordered by King Leopold to cease fire on 28 May.

b meanwhile, the Germans launched their main attack under von Rundstedt on a weakly-held section of the French line in the Ardennes forest, where the French General Staff had believed the German panzers could not penetrate the thick woodlands. The Germans proved them wrong, and used new tank tactics which had been thought up by British tank experts between the wars, but which had not been adopted by the British Army. Instead of being scattered among the infantry battalions to support them, the German tanks were concentrated in panzer divisions, which were used to force a breach in the enemy's front line. Then, helped by dive-bombers, and in some cases by spies and parachute troops, the panzers wrought havoc among the enemy's headquarters, supplies and communications, securing an easy passage for the German infantry divisions which followed.

Fig. 41   The German 'Blitzkreig' May-June 1940.

c thus, a few days after the break-through, the Germans had split the Allied forces in two by reaching the English Channel. The British Commander, Gort, saw that the only chance of saving his troops was evacuation, and he ordered them to retreat to Dunkirk. Here, in the week 27 May to 4 June, a third of a million Allied troops were taken off the French shore to Britain by the Royal Navy, helped by small coastal and river craft from all over southern England.

d Mussolini, convinced that a German victory was certain, determined to seize the 'chance of a thousand years' as his son-in-law and Foreign Minister Ciano put it, and declared war on Britain and France on 10 June, hoping for valuable gains at the coming peace conference. In Africa, his troops invaded Egypt from Libya, but were halted and thrown back by General Wavell's forces in December.

e after Dunkirk, the Germans launched an all-out attack against the remaining Allied armies in France. On 13 June they captured Paris, and on the 16th Marshal Pétain, the hero of Verdun in the First World War, became French Premier, and asked the Germans for an armistice. This was signed on 22 June at Compiègne, in the same railway carriage that had been used for the signing of the armistice of 11 November 1918. This was followed by a similar agreement between France and Italy.

f France agreed to disarm her forces, and handed over the whole of northern France and her Atlantic coast to German control. Pétain set up a new government at Vichy, and soon became 'Head of State' with the pro-German Pierre Laval as his Prime Minister. Meanwhile, General Charles de Gaulle had arrived in London, and called upon all Frenchmen to join his 'Free French' movement, determined to continue the struggle against Germany.

4 The Battle of Britain:

a as Britain ignored his offers of peace, Hitler now planned to invade her in 'Operation Sealion'. Before this could take place, control of the air over southern England was vital. Therefore, he ordered Goering, head of the German Luftwaffe, to destroy the RAF. This Goering promised to do.

b RAF fighters had done well against the Germans in the French campaign, but had been outnumbered and Air Chief Marshal Dowding, their Commander, had had to keep back enough squadrons to ensure the defence of Britain.

Fighter Command's main weapon was the eight-gun fighter, the 'Hurricane' and the 'Spitfire'. The pilots were well-trained.

Vital in the battle was the chain of radar stations round the south-eastern coast of Britain. These told ground controllers the height, direction, speed and rough number of attacking aircraft, and allowed them to direct the fighter aircraft where and when they were needed.

c the Luftwaffe, fresh from its triumphs in Europe, was confident of victory. Its main fighter was the excellent Messerschmidt 109, a match for the Spitfire. Its bombers were less impressive. The Stuka dive-bomber and the Heinkel 111 and Dornier 17 medium bombers were weak in defensive armament, and needed heavy fighter escort.

The Germans had the disadvantage that as most of the fighting took place over Britain, British aircrew forced to parachute from their planes would be able to rejoin the struggle, but Germans in the same position would become prisoners of war.

d German attacks started in July, and reached their peak in August and September. Both sides lost heavily, the Germans more so. Goering made the mistake of switching his targets. He started with attacks on the radar stations, then switched to Fighter Command airfields. Just when these had nearly succeeded, he switched to attacks on London and other cities, stung by a British raid on Berlin.

e in mid-September Hitler realised that Germany had lost this battle, and called off Operation Sealion.

With the longer nights the Germans switched their attacks to night raids, which they carried out in the winter of 1940–1 almost without loss at first, as the British night-fighters had as yet no airborne radar. London,

Plymouth, Liverpool and many other towns suffered in this 'Blitz'. One of the worst raids was on Coventry on the night of 14 November.

5 The war at sea:

a the German successes on land meant that the western coast of Europe from northern Norway to the south-west of France was available to them as bases for U-boats and aircraft. This was very serious for Britain, and her shipping losses started to increase steeply.

b the French collapse meant that their navy might fall into German hands. To prevent this the Royal Navy attacked the French Fleet at its base at Oran in North Africa and sank much of it on 3 July.

c elsewhere in the Mediterranean, the Italian Fleet showed no wish to come out and fight, so carrier-borne aircraft of the British Fleet attacked it at its base, Taranto, in November, and inflicted heavy losses. The British base at Malta came under heavy air attack, which continued for over two years.

6 Other countries:

a Stalin was dismayed at Hitler's quick successes in the west. For Russia's protection he ordered his forces to occupy the Republics of Estonia, Latvia and Lithuania on the Baltic, and forced Rumania to hand over Bessarabia.

b in September Japan signed a ten-year treaty of friendship with Germany and Italy. This seemed to bring war in the Far East nearer for a hard-pressed Britain, especially as in June Japan forced France to hand over Indo-China.

c the USA introduced conscription and began to build up her forces. Despite isolationist opposition, Roosevelt helped Britain in two ways.

The troops evacuated from Dunkirk had had to leave behind nearly all their equipment, even their rifles. Therefore in June America sold Britain a large number of rifles, machine guns and ammunition.

To help combat the U-boat menace, in September the USA sent fifty old destroyers in return for 99-year leases on bases in Newfoundland and the West Indies.

Fig. 42   Early British radar. In the 'secret war' to develop new scientific weapons such as improved radar, Britain and the USA won important victories over Germany. Hitler's secret weapons' (the V1 and V2) came too late to save him. The British intelligence network also scored over its German counterpart. For instance, long after the war ended, it was revealed that the British 'Ultra' organisation had broken the vital German 'Enigma' code when the war started, which meant that Britain had been able to intercept many important messages.

Fig. 43   Air raid damage in Coventry, 1940.

With the entry of Russia, Japan and the USA into the war, it now became world-wide. British forces fought the Germans and Italians on land in Africa and in the Balkans.

1 The British and Allied Eighth Army in Egypt continued to drive the Italians back into Libya, and the Germans were forced to come to Italy's help. Hitler sent General Rommel, who later was to become famous as the 'Desert Fox' because of his skill in desert warfare, and his 'Afrika Korps' of German troops to Libya.

Rommel drove the Allied forces, weakened by the need to send help to Greece, back into Egypt. Tobruk, however, held out against the Germans for eight months until relieved by an Allied counter-offensive from Egypt in December.

British and Allied forces helped the Abyssinians to reconquer their country from Italy by the end of the year, and the Emperor Haile Selassie was able to return from exile. Thus Italy lost her East African Empire.

2 In the Balkans, Hitler 'persuaded' Hungary, Rumania and Bulgaria to join the Axis powers, as Germany and Italy called themselves. (Mussolini had said that the world would 'revolve on a Rome-Berlin axis'.)

However, a revolution in Yugoslavia brought the downfall of the pro-Axis Regent Paul, and his replacement by King Peter II. Hitler now decided to crush Yugoslavia and Greece. This took only a few weeks in April. The Yugoslav capital, Belgrade, was flattened by German bombers in 'Operation Punishment' and the help which Britain had hurriedly sent to Greece proved not enough.

However, the brave fight put up by these two countries delayed Hitler's coming attack on Russia for six vital weeks of spring and summer weather. Also, the Yugoslavs formed groups of partisans who continued the fight against the Germans in the mountains. Among their leaders was the future President Tito.

3 The Germans followed this up with a successful airborne attack on the island of Crete in May. Here, the invaders suffered such heavy losses that Hitler called off a proposed similar attack on Malta, which however continued to suffer heavy air raids.

4 Hitler now felt free to go ahead with 'Operation Barbarossa', his invasion of Russia.

For this he had made careful plans. Air and land forces were moved from the west, and took up their attack positions along the Russian frontier. With them were forces from Hitler's allies, Italians, Finns, Hungarians, Rumanians and Bulgars. All told, Hitler's generals led about three million men on the 'eastern front'. Yet Hitler gambled, foolishly, on a victory over Russia in 1941, and made no plans for a winter campaign.

On 22 June, without warning, the Axis forces attacked, on a front which stretched from the Arctic to the Black Sea. At first, the Russians were taken by surprise, and everywhere they were driven back. The Germans made three main thrusts, towards Leningrad, Moscow and the Caucasus. The Russians lost hundreds of thousands of prisoners, and vast stocks of equipment, yet the Axis powers were unable to secure a victory that would knock Russia out of the war.

5 By early December, the Red Army was still fighting, and winter brought the invaders to a halt. In the north, Leningrad had begun a siege that was to last until 1943, and cause terrible suffering among the civilian population. In the south, the Germans had captured the Ukraine, with its important cities of Kiev and Kharkov. In the centre, they were only twenty miles from Moscow. Here, the Russians counter-attacked and drove the Wehrmacht back, the first real defeat the German Army had suffered in the war so far. Then stalemate set in along the eastern front until spring.

6 Time was on the side of the Russians. They had evacuated hundreds of arms factories to safe areas behind the Ural mountains. Vast new armies were being trained and equipped. Behind the German lines bands of guerrillas operated, and became a growing menace as the war went on.

Help came from abroad as Britain, and later the United States, began to send huge amounts of aircraft, guns, tanks and raw materials to Russia.

Also the Germans had not expected, and

were not equipped for, a winter campaign.
They even lacked warm clothing. Thus their
troops suffered dreadfully, for instance from
frostbite. As the war went on, the Red Army
learned from its defeats, and proved a match for
the Wehrmacht in battle. Hitler was forced to
send more and more men to fight and die on the
dreaded 'Ostfront' as the Russian front was
called.

7 Hitler's rule in Europe:

a this varied somewhat in severity. It was
harshest in eastern Europe and occupied
Russia, where the people were regarded by
their conquerors as 'Untermenschen' or subhumans.

In one or two countries, e.g. Denmark, the
Germans aimed at first at a 'model' occupation, and tried to win over the people by a
show of friendship.

b generally, however, occupation by German
forces was followed at once by rounding-up
'anti-Nazi elements'. These might be known
Communists or anybody who had spoken out
against Nazism in the past. These, together
with Jews, would be sent off to Germany or
Poland to the dreaded concentration camps,
and usually never heard of again.

c there would be some 'quislings' or col-
laborators. These would be put into power,
under a 'puppet' government set up to work
with Germany. In some countries men
volunteered to fight for the Germans, especially against Russia.

d the German authorities would help themselves to machinery, farm tools, raw materials,
food, etc. which would be sent back to the
Reich, even if the local people starved as a
result. Even art treasures were pillaged.
Goering, for instance, became notorious for
stealing paintings and sculptures from all
over occupied Europe. Some factories were
not stripped, but were made to produce goods
for the Nazi war effort.

e all over Europe men and women were
conscripted as virtual slaves and sent to
Germany to work in the arms factories. At
one time, it has been estimated, there were
seven million of these in Germany.

Fig. 44 North Africa and the Mediterranean in the Second World War.

f of course, resistance movements grew up everywhere. To keep a check on these and enforce Nazi rule, the dreaded Gestapo or secret police had its agents everywhere. Anyone unfortunate enough to be suspected would be arrested and subjected to the most brutal tortures at the Gestapo's hands.

g the Germans often took hostages from the local people, and shot them if any anti-German activities, e.g. sabotage, took place. In some places, as in the Czech village of Lidice, whole communities were butchered.

h despite all the Germans' efforts, the resistance movements fought on. Underground newspapers were printed and circulated, while many patriots risked death to listen to BBC broadcasts. Agents and arms were parachuted into occupied countries from Britain. The Resistance helped the Allied war effort in two main ways.

Firstly, vital information was sent back to the Allies e.g. on the development of Hitler's 'secret weapons'.

Secondly, acts of sabotage, such as derailment of German troop trains, were carried out. Towards the end of the war the Resistance

was fighting the Germans in pitched battles in Yugoslavia and France. In France the Maquis (as the Resistance was called) played a vital part in stopping German reinforcements from reaching the Normandy beach-heads until it was too late (June 1944).

8 The war spread in December to the Far East. The USA had become increasingly hostile to Japan over the matter of the 'China Incident'. Along with Britain and the Netherlands (who ruled the Dutch East Indies, now Indonesia), the Americans threatened to cut off Japan's supplies of oil and other raw materials. This would have brought Japan to her knees, and so General Tojo, the Prime Minister, and his Cabinet, decided on war.

Japan's leaders believed that with Britain fully occupied in Europe, and the other colonial powers, France and the Netherlands, defeated by Germany, the USA would be unwilling to fight Japan virtually single-handed, and that isolationist feelings in the States would be strong enough to force Roosevelt to make peace if faced with a string of Japanese victories.

9 Accordingly the Japanese Navy planned a torpedo and bomb attack by its carrier planes on the American Pacific Fleet at its base, Pearl Harbor, in the Hawaiian Islands. The attack was thoroughly rehearsed, and when launched

Fig. 45   The Japanese attack on Pearl Harbor, 7 December 1941.

on 7 December, proved a great success. Several American battleships and smaller vessels were sunk, and this crippled the American Fleet for a few months, while Japanese forces roamed the western Pacific almost at will, and carried all before them. (Yet, luckily for the Americans, their aircraft carriers had not been in Pearl Harbor at the time of the attack and so had escaped unharmed.)

10 However, Tojo and his Ministers had misjudged the situation badly. Pearl Harbor united Americans of all opinions behind Roosevelt in a determination to fight until victory was gained.

Already, in March, Roosevelt had persuaded Congress to pass the Lend-Lease Act, which allowed the American Government to 'lend' military equipment of all kinds to any country whose defence seemed important to the defence of the United States. Britain and all America's allies benefited enormously from this act as the war went on.

11 The day after Pearl Harbor, the USA and Britain (followed by the Dominions, China, and the Netherlands Government in exile) declared war on Japan.

Four days after Pearl Harbor, Germany and Italy declared war on the United States.

12 At first, thanks to their excellent seamanship, fanatical courage, and equipment, such as the 'long lance' torpedo and 'Zero' fighter, which were better than anything the Allies had at the time in that area, the Japanese swept all before them.

Japanese forces invaded Malaya to attack the British naval base at Singapore. The battleship 'Prince of Wales' and the old battlecruiser 'Repulse', sent to attack the invasion fleet, were sunk in the Straits of Malacca by air attack on 10 December. Hong Kong fell on the 25th, and Japanese forces invaded the American-held Philippine Islands.

13 In Britain, Churchill saw that the entry of the USA into the war on the Allies' side made victory certain, though there would be heavy sacrifices to make first.

In 1941 Britain continued to suffer German air attack, but on nothing like the scale of late 1940, especially when the Luftwaffe began to transfer many of its squadrons to the east for the invasion of Russia. The RAF replaced the fighters lost in 1940, and began to build up a large force of four-engined bombers for attacks on Germany.

14 At sea, losses from U-boat attacks were high, though even before her entry into the war the USA had helped protect convoys against this menace.

In the Mediterranean the Royal Navy inflicted a defeat on the Italians off Cape Matapan.

In May, the new German giant battleship 'Bismarck' left its base and sailed into the Atlantic to attack Allied shipping. Churchill ordered that she must be sunk at all costs. However, in her first encounter with British ships, she sank the pride of the Royal Navy, the battlecruiser 'Hood', and forced 'Hood's' companion 'Prince of Wales' to retire damaged. Three days later, 'Bismarck's' steering was crippled by a torpedo hit from the British carrier 'Ark Royal's' aircraft. The battleships 'Rodney' and 'King George V' caught up with 'Bismarck' and sent her to the bottom.

D 1942

This year started with a string of defeats for the Allies, yet it also saw the turning of the tide against the Axis powers and ended with important Allied victories. Britain's main effort against Germany took place in North Africa, in the Atlantic, and in the air over Germany.

1 In North Africa, the Germans, led by Rommel, took the offensive in May and drove the Allied forces back. By now the Eighth Army or 'Desert Rats' included, besides British troops, French, Poles, Australians, New Zealanders, South Africans, Indians and others.

Tobruk fell to the Afrika Korps in June, and Rommel was not stopped until he reached El Alamein, well inside Egypt. However, strong reinforcements arrived for the Eighth Army, and a new Commander, General Montgomery, took over. In October the Allies went over to the attack, and Montgomery threw back Rommel's German and Italian forces at the battle of El Alamein.

2 On 8 November, a British and American army, led by the American General Eisenhower, landed in French North Africa (Operation Torch), which was occupied by pro-Vichy French forces. Their Commander, Admiral Darlan, signed an armistice a few days later, which led the Germans to invade unoccupied France.

3 The Axis forces in Africa were now in a difficult position, between two Allied armies. Yet Hitler sent reinforcements, and not until May 1943 were the last of the German and Italian troops in North Africa forced to surrender in Tunisia.

This meant the lifting of the siege of Malta, which had suffered heavy air attack for over two years, and which was awarded the George Cross for its heroism.

4 At sea the 'Battle of the Atlantic', as Churchill called it, caused heavy loss to both sides:

a the German Admiral Doenitz developed new tactics for his increased force of submarines, using them in 'wolf packs' instead of singly against the Allied convoys. Yet the supply of troops, war material and food from America to Britain grew steadily, as did supplies to Russia.

Fig. 46 'Lancaster' of Bomber Command, RAF. The German Luftwaffe failed to develop a similar heavy bomber force, believing that in a short Blitzkrieg war such planes would not be needed.

b the northern convoy route to Russia's ports of Murmansk and Archangel was one of the most dangerous. Here the convoys often met dreadful weather, and faced attack not only from U-boats, but from German shore-based aircraft and surface ships.

As summer approached, the nights, which had given some cover, shortened, and thus attacks on the convoys continued almost around the clock. Indeed, at one time, the Allies had to stop the Russian convoys for a while, much to Stalin's annoyance.

c in February, the German battlecruisers 'Scharnhorst' and 'Gneisenau' escaped from the French port of Brest to bases in Germany by sailing through the English Channel. That they should get away with this was a big blow to British prestige, yet in fact both were put out of action for a time by damage from mines, and had been a more serious threat to convoys when based at Brest.

5 In the air, the RAF sent growing forces of bombers to attack Germany at night. Most famous and successful of the machines was the 'Lancaster'.

Before the war, some had believed that air power alone could bring victory. A steady aerial bombardment of an enemy's towns and cities, it was believed, would force him to ask for peace. World War Two proved this wrong as far as attack with conventional (i.e. high explosive, not atomic) bombs was concerned.

As the war went on, Bomber Command of the RAF, led by Air Chief Marshal Sir Arthur Harris, was able to send as many as a thousand aircraft to attack a single German city in one night, but the Germans stood up to it. Bombing at night was not very accurate, especially in the early stages of the war. Later, however, heavy damage was caused to Germany's war effort, her factories and railways.

Yet war production in Germany increased in 1943 and 1944, when the RAF offensive was at its height. Many critics of Harris's policy of massive raids on German cities say that this showed that Bomber Command was misused. On the other hand, it seems certain that without the heavy air raids (in which the Americans with their 'Flying Fortress' and 'Liberator' bombers joined as the war went on, usually attacking by daylight) German production, and development of secret weapons, would have been even more effective.

6 On the Russian front, the Germans met disaster:

  a at first, a German summer offensive was very successful in southern Russia. It aimed at securing for Germany the oil of the Caucasus. By August, the German forces had advanced hundreds of miles, and the Caucasus seemed to be theirs. In September they reached Stalingrad, an important industrial and communications centre, on the River Volga.

  b here the German advance was checked in desperate street fighting. Both sides threw reinforcements into the battle, then, in late November, the Russians attacked north and south-east of the city in a vast 'pincer movement' designed to cut off the German attackers (the Sixth Army, led by General von Paulus).

  c although asked by his Generals to allow a retreat from Stalingrad before it was too late, Hitler stubbornly refused. As a result, the Sixth Army was cut off by the Russians, and soon began to run short of food, medical supplies and ammunition in the terrible Russian winter. Despite heavy losses, they held out until February before surrendering. Stalingrad had cost the Germans a quarter of a million men.

Fig. 47   Europe in 1942, showing alliances.

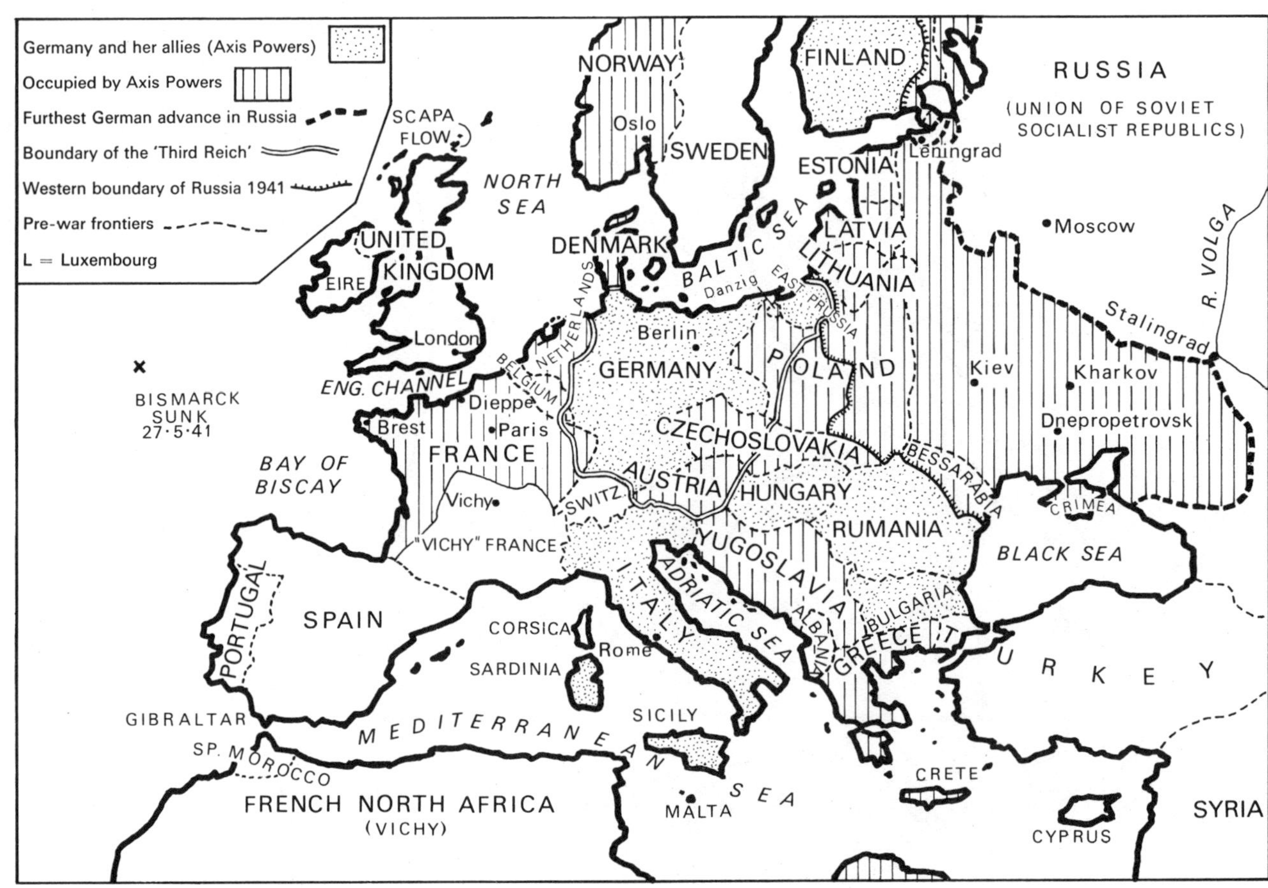

7 In the Far East, Japan, intent on securing the tin and rubber of Malaya and the oil of the Dutch East Indies, scored great successes, yet her tide of conquest was halted:

a the Japanese invasion of Malaya continued unchecked, and reached a triumphant climax when the British naval base at Singapore fell, with 60 000 prisoners, on 15 February.

b the Japanese Army then advanced into Burma, which fell by the end of May.

c following a naval victory at the Battle of the Java Sea, Japanese forces landed in the Dutch East Indies, which were quickly overrun.

d in the Philippine Islands, American and Filipino troops put up a brave resistance at Bataan and on the island of Corregidor, which did not surrender until 6 May. The American Commander, General MacArthur, was taken off the island by submarine, his last words before leaving being, 'I shall return'.

e further Japanese forces captured the Solomon Islands and northern New Guinea, thus seeming to threaten Australia.

f so far, Japan had enjoyed six months of victory. Now she was checked. In May, a Japanese invasion force was turned back at the Battle of the Coral Sea, the first of a new kind of battle where the opposing ships never saw each other, and all the fighting was done by aircraft operating from carriers. This was the first real check the Japanese had so far suffered.

g the following month at the Battle of Midway, the Japanese Fleet met with heavy defeat at the hands of a much weaker American force, losing four of their prized carriers.

h in August, US Marines recaptured the island of Guadalcanal, though the Japanese tried hard to retake it, and there was much bitter fighting before it was secure in American hands.

Fig. 48   The war in the Pacific, 1941-5.

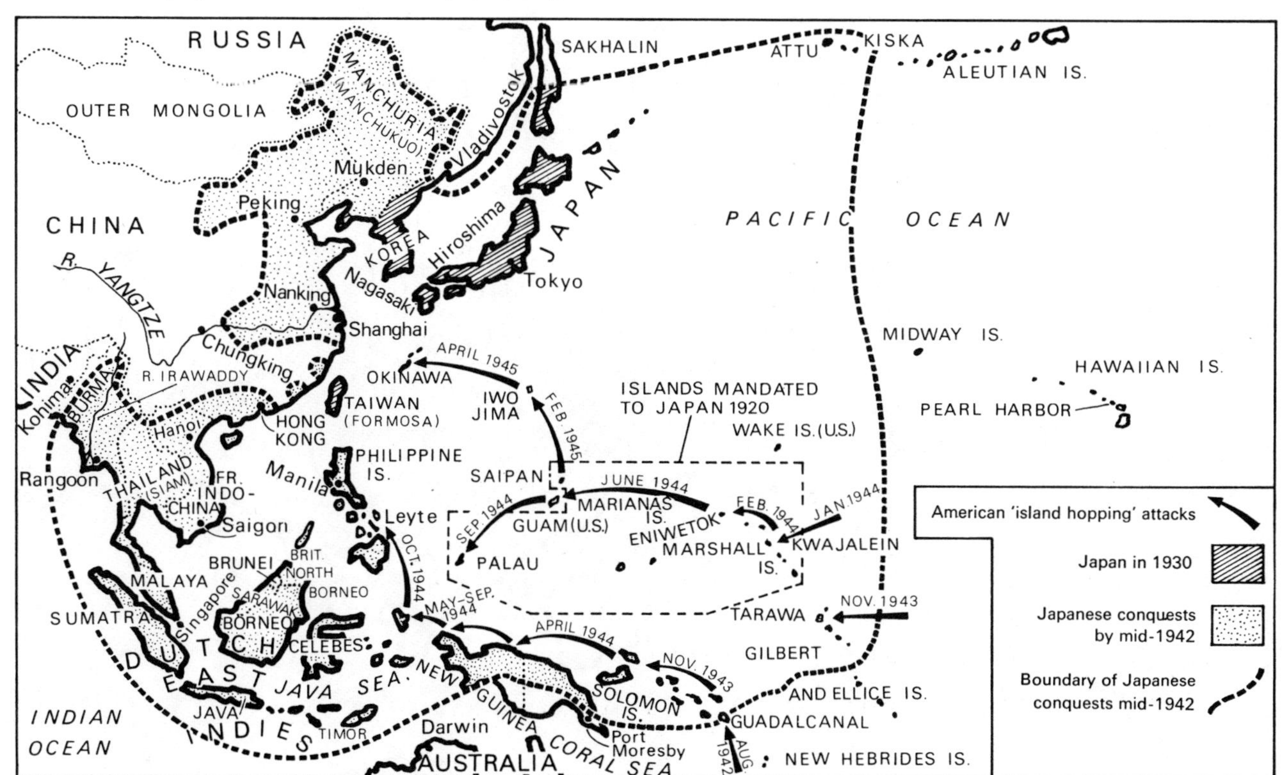

E 1943

This year saw the Axis and Japanese forces on the defensive and in retreat. Britain's main effort on land was her part in the invasion of Italy, while at sea the submarine menace was largely overcome, and in the air the bombing of Germany was stepped up.

1 Following the surrender in May of the last Axis forces in Africa, British and American forces invaded Sicily on 9 July. The run of Italian defeats caused Mussolini's fall from power (see Ch. 4), and Italy asked for an armistice.

However, the Germans were quick to occupy Italy, as Allied troops discovered when they landed on the Italian mainland in September. They tried to outflank German resistance by a landing at Salerno, but the Germans reacted quickly, and the operation came close to disaster before the Allies were able to advance and capture Naples.

2 1943 saw the defeat of the U-boat. Many more British and American convoy escorts came into use. 'Hunter-killer' groups of these were detached from close escort duties to seek out and destroy the German submarines wherever they were. Long-range Allied aircraft were now able to protect convoys on the whole of their journey across the Atlantic.

3 Bomber Command increased its offensive against Germany. The centre of Hamburg was destroyed in a fire storm during one such raid, and Berlin came under almost nightly attack at one stage.

4 On the Russian front, the German forces were driven steadily back:

a early in the year, Leningrad was relieved, and the last Germans at Stalingrad surrendered.

b Russia's armies, helped by masses of war material from Britain and the United States, began to match the Germans in skill and to overwhelm them in numbers.

c the Germans opened spring and summer offensives, but these scored nothing like the successes of earlier years. Instead, the Red Army checked them, and by the end of the year the Wehrmacht was being steadily driven back, though still fighting on Russian soil.

5 In the Pacific, the Americans built up vast forces, under the supreme command of General MacArthur. This was a sea war, involving vast distances, and MacArthur devised the strategy of 'island-hopping'.

America built up 'task forces' of transport ships carrying troops, marines and all their equipment, protected by strong naval forces of battleships, cruisers, destroyers, and most important of all, aircraft carriers, which also provided the air support for attacks on Japanese ships and land bases. The task forces were to be used to capture suitable bases along the Americans' line of advance to Japan itself. This would form a chain of islands in American hands. Many Japanese garrisons were cut off and left to starve ('wither on the vine' as MacArthur put it). This advance started in 1943, and speeded up the following year.

Fig. 49   The Russian front, 1943. The Red Flag flies over a ruined Stalingrad.

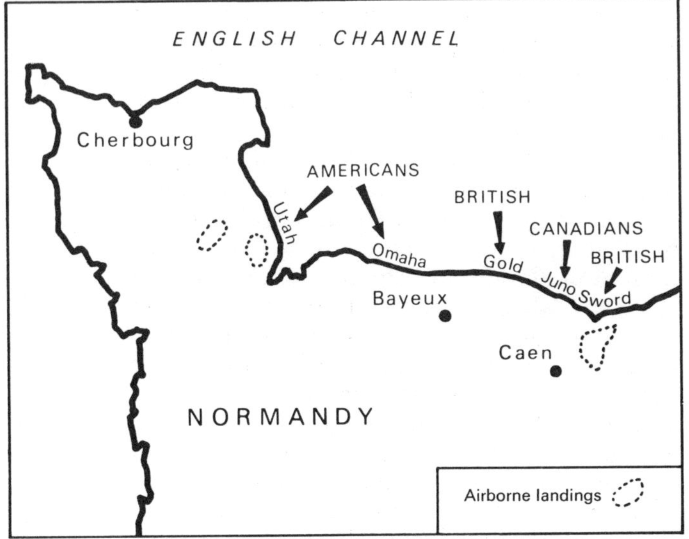

Fig. 50   *D-Day landings, 6 June 1944.*

Fig. 51   *American troops coming ashore during the D-Day landings in Normandy.*

F 1944

The end of this year saw Germany and Japan fighting for their lives.

1 Britain's war effort was now far exceeded by that of the USA, and it was clear that in the coming invasion of Europe, American troops would outnumber British. Thus in the planning for this invasion, called operation 'Overlord', Eisenhower was named as Supreme Commander.

2 Meanwhile, Italy was the scene of bitter fighting:

  a in February, Allied forces tried to outflank the Germans by landing at Anzio. As at Salerno, the Germans counter-attacked strongly, but without success.

  b Monte Cassino proved difficult for the Allies to capture, and fell only after Allied aircraft had bombed the centuries-old monastery of St Benedict.

  c on 4 June, Rome fell to the Allies, but further progress up the peninsula proved difficult.

3 On 'D-Day' (6 June) Allied invasion armies landed on the coast of Normandy in northern France, under the command of General Montgomery:

  a this, the biggest amphibious (land and sea) operation in history, had been successfully and well planned. Much had been learned by the Allies from the failure of the Dieppe raid in 1942, when several thousand British and Canadian troops had suffered heavy losses through lack of sufficient air and sea support.

  b a huge force of troops, guns, tanks, aircraft and ships had been built up in southern England for the invasion. On the day, 4 000 ships carried the men and their equipment across the Channel.

  c strict precautions had been taken to deceive the Germans as to the spot where the blow would fall. Hitler believed it would come in the Calais area, where the sea crossing was shortest. On the eve of D-Day, Allied ships cruised off the French coast there, while in the air, specially-trained bomber crews dropped strips of 'window' (aluminium foil) to deceive the German radar into thinking a large air attack was about to take place.

Hitler refused to believe that the Normandy attack was the main one.

d control of the air was almost completely in the hands of the Allies. In the weeks before the invasion, road and rail bridges in northern France had been systematically destroyed by bombing so as to hinder the flow of German reinforcements to the battle area.

The coast to be attacked had been carefully photographed from the air, and enemy positions noted. These received heavy fire from the Allied warships and aircraft before the invaders landed.

e at sea, defences against U-boats were completely successful, so that not a single man of the invasion force was lost at sea from such attack.

f one objection to the Normandy coast as a landing-place was its lack of large harbours for the forces and supplies that would follow in the weeks after D-Day. To overcome this shortage, two large artificial harbours, called 'Mulberries' had been prepared. For petrol supply, a special pipe line under the ocean (Pluto) was ready to lay from Britain to Normandy.

g thus when the Allied forces attacked by sea and air on 6 June, casualties were much lighter than many had feared, though the Americans were held up for a time at Omaha Beach. By the evening of D-Day it was clear that the landings had been successful. At first, however, progress was slower than had been hoped for. The build-up of Allied strength went on for several weeks, and then in July the Americans, led by General Patton, broke out near St Lo, and spread rapidly across France.

4 Now, German resistance crumbled, and helped by the French resistance movement, the Maquis, Allied troops advanced quickly. In August Paris was freed from the Germans, and in September Brussels was liberated. More Allied troops were landed in the south of France in August, and linked up with the armies in the north.

5 Yet the Germans were able to halt the Allied advance in the autumn, and even to counter-attack. Although the Allies reached the German frontier in places in September, the Germans put up a stiff fight and halted the advance.

An attempt by British Paratroops to seize the Rhine crossings at Arnhem in Holland failed in September.

6 In December, the Germans launched their last offensive in the west in the Ardennes, the 'Battle of the Bulge'. This attack was planned in great secrecy by the Germans under von Rundstedt, and took advantage of bad weather, which grounded most Allied aircraft. At first the attack was successful, but it was halted after ten days, the Germans having lost heavily in men and equipment.

7 On the Eastern Front, the Germans suffered defeat everywhere. Hitler made matters worse by insisting that his armies should not retreat a single metre, and ordering officers who broke this rule to be shot. This deprived his troops of freedom to manoeuvre in the face of Russian attacks, with the result that tens of thousands of German soldiers were captured by the Red Army.

The Ukraine, eastern Poland, Lithuania, Latvia and Estonia were freed by the Russians. Rumania and Bulgaria surrendered, and Yugoslavia was freed. By the end of the year the Russians were on the borders of Germany itself.

8 Germany's position was now hopeless. Once again she was in the nightmare position of fighting on two fronts (or three including Italy). The USA and Russia possessed almost limitless resources of men and war materials. The Reich was bombed, almost without stopping, by the Americans in the daytime and the RAF at night. The once-powerful Luftwaffe was desperately short of fuel and of trained pilots, and was swamped by the sheer number of Allied aircraft.

9 Realisation of this led a group of German officers, led by von Stulpnagel, to plan to assassinate Hitler in the bomb plot of 20 July 1944. However, the bomb placed close to Hitler during a conference at his headquarters in East Prussia failed to kill him, and the plot came to nothing. The conspirators were ruthlessly hunted down and punished, among them being Field-Marshal Rommel, who was allowed to commit suicide.

10 In the Far East, the Japanese Premier Tojo was forced to resign in August 1944.

American forces advanced steadily across the Pacific, and invaded the Philippine Islands in October. Here the Japanese launched their last large-scale counter-attack by sea and air, and were heavily defeated in the Battle of Leyte Gulf.

In Burma, 'Chindit' troops under General Orde Wingate were specially trained to land and operate behind the Japanese lines, with great success.

On the borders of India and Burma, a Japanese attempt to invade India was defeated at Kohima by the British Fourteenth Army, led by General Slim, under the control of Admiral Lord Louis Mountbatten.

G 1945

1 The downfall of Germany:

a in January and February the Russians launched heavy attacks, driving the Wehrmacht out of Poland. Soon the Red Army was within fifty kilometres of Berlin.

b in February, Allied forces attacked the Germans in the west, crossing the Rhine in early March.

c in April and early May German resistance collapsed. First to surrender were their forces in northern Italy (where Mussolini was captured by Communist partisans and shot), commanded by von Kesselring.

Fig. 52   German Commanders surrender their forces to Field-Marshal Montgomery in May 1945.

d German radio announced that Hitler was dead. As the Russians entered Berlin, he and Eva Braun had been married, then committed suicide in the Führerbunker, his underground headquarters in the gardens of the Reich Chancellery. Their bodies had then been burnt. Hitler named Admiral Doenitz to succeed him as Führer.

2 By 7 May all the German armies in Europe had surrendered. Those in north Germany did so to Montgomery at his headquarters on Luneberg Heath.

V-E Day (short for victory in Europe) was proclaimed by the Allies on 8 May, and was followed by great rejoicing in all the Allied capitals.

3 A fate similar to that of Germany awaited Japan. Despite fanatical resistance, US Marines captured the islands of Iwo Jima and Okinawa, which gave the Americans air bases on Japan's doorstep. In desperation, the Japanese launched heavy Kamikaze (suicide plane) attacks on the American Fleets. The volunteer pilots were locked into their cockpits, having vowed to crash into an enemy ship. Japan was driven to this by a shortage of aviation fuel and trained crews. These attacks had some success, but failed to stop American operations, as by July, Japan was suffering heavy aerial bombardment from their carrier- and land-based aircraft.

Japan's position was now hopeless. Cut off from her sources of raw materials, e.g. oil, in south-east Asia, she had no chance of replacing the aircraft or ships lost to the Americans. Yet the invasion of Japan would have been a bloody business, as President Truman realised when he authorised the use of the atomic bomb on two Japanese cities.

4 After the first of these was dropped on Hiroshima on 6 August, Russia (which had so far been at peace with Japan) declared war and invaded Japanese-held Manchuria.

The dropping of the second A-bomb, on Nagasaki on 9 August, led the Japanese Cabinet to advise the Emperor Hirohito to order his forces, at sea, on land and in the air, to surrender to the Allies, which they did on 14 August. A peace treaty was signed on 2 September, by representatives of the Allies and the

Japanese Government, on the deck of the US battleship 'Missouri' in Tokyo Bay. General MacArthur presided.

H Britain in the Second World War

1 Air raids. When these started they caused heavy damage, in three main stages: the 'Battle of Britain' July–September 1940; the winter blitz of 1940–1; and the V1 (flying bomb) and V2 (rocket) attacks, 1944–5. London in particular, Liverpool, Plymouth, Coventry and other places suffered heavy damage. 60 000 people were killed. There was not the panic that had been expected, but many houses were destroyed or badly damaged.

2 Rationing. Most foods (though not bread), sweets, clothing and even furniture were rationed. Food prices were subsidised and controlled by the government to keep them down. Britain's farmers were encouraged to grow more. Special foods, e.g. dried milk and vitamins, were issued free or at a low charge to expectant mothers and young children.

A big advertising campaign was run by the government to educate people to eat a balanced diet. Though the ration seemed low at times, e.g. one fresh egg a week, it was always enough for health. The result was that the people of Britain were better fed than ever before. Malnutrition among schoolchildren fell.

3 Manpower. The government took firm steps to direct the people of Britain for the war effort. Over four million men were called up for the forces. Women served, as in the First World War, with the army, navy and air force, and in the Women's Land Army. They were employed in millions in factories. The government took steps to stop people leaving jobs that were important for the war effort, e.g. the railways. Thus for the first time since 1920 there was full employment.

4 Foreign trade and investments. Exports fell, partly because Britain's factories were making war material for the forces; partly because of difficulties over importing raw materials, e.g. cotton; and partly because of shipping difficulties, such as the sinking of merchant ships by enemy submarines.

Therefore, to pay for imports, Britain had to sell many of her investments abroad, and borrow large amounts of money from other countries. Both these steps were to have serious results after the war.

5 Finance. The war cost huge amounts of money. It was paid for by increased taxation and borrowing.

Increases in taxes paid for about half of the cost of the war. Income tax went up to 50p in the pound, and surtax to 97½p in the pound. A new 'purchase tax' was levied on a wide range of goods, e.g. clothing, toys and furniture.

All classes of people were encouraged to lend to the government through National Savings, such as War Bonds, Savings Certificates and Savings Stamps.

6 The mood of the people. The war caused the British people to question much of what had happened pre-war and to demand a much better future. Thus during the war a Ministry of Reconstruction was set up to make plans for when the war ended, the Beveridge Report laid the foundation for the 'Welfare State', and an important Education Act was passed in 1944.

After peace was made with Germany, but before the defeat of Japan, the general election of 1945 resulted in a clear Labour victory.

Fig. 53   Ration book issued to King George VI.

THE PEACE SETTLEMENT, 1945

A Preparations for Peace

1 The heads of the leading Allied nations met several times during the war to plan its progress and to discuss arrangements for the peace settlement when the war ended.

2 The most important of the wartime conferences of Allied leaders took place at Yalta in the Crimea in February 1945:

    a Churchill, Roosevelt and Stalin represented Britain, the USA and Russia.

    b Roosevelt persuaded Churchill to agree to halt the advance of the western armies in positions far short of Churchill's original intentions. This would allow a Russian advance into central Europe, e.g. Germany and Austria.

    c Russia was to be allowed to keep the Baltic states of Estonia, Latvia and Lithuania, which she had annexed in 1940, and Bessarabia. Her frontier with Poland was to be advanced westwards to the so-called 'Curzon Line'.

    d in Poland itself, a government approved by Stalin was to be set up.

    e Poland and Russia were to share East Prussia (taken from Germany) at the same time as Poland's border with Germany proper was moved westwards to the line of the Oder and Neisse rivers.

    f Stalin agreed to declare war on Japan in the near future.

    g the outlines of the peace settlement with Japan were agreed upon.

    h the statesmen agreed that a United Nations' Organization should be set up.

B The Peace Settlement

1 Following the defeat of Germany, a conference was held at Potsdam (outside Berlin) in July and August 1945. This confirmed the Yalta agreements, and the peace settlement to be imposed upon Germany.

By then Harry S. Truman, who had become President on Roosevelt's death in April, represented the USA. Churchill no longer represented Britain, as the Labour leader Clement Attlee had become Prime Minister, following the Conservatives' defeat in the general election a few weeks before. Only Stalin remained of the 'Big Three' who had met at Yalta.

2 The Conference agreed that Germany should be split into four zones, each with an army of occupation, British, American, Russian, and French. Berlin was in the Russian zone, but would be divided among the four Allies.

Germany's war industries, e.g. Krupp's of Essen, were to be broken up, and the machinery shared among the Allies in reparations.

German war criminals, whether civilian Nazis or leaders of the armed forces, were to be brought to trial. This led to the famous Nuremberg trials.

3 The settlement with Japan:

    a Japan was forced to give up all her conquests on the mainland of Asia and in the Pacific Ocean. Korea became two independent Republics (which were supposed to become one). Formosa was returned to China, and the southern half of the island of Sakhalin was handed over to Russia.

    b as in Germany, war criminals, including Tojo, were tried and received sentences of death or imprisonment.

    c the Emperor Hirohito kept his position as head of state, but gave up his claim to be a god, the 'Son of Heaven', becoming instead a constitutional Monarch with very limited powers, on the British model. A democratic Constitution was set up, with a Parliament on western lines, while the press and education were freed from government censorship.

    d American occupation forces were to be stationed in Japan.

4 Other countries:

    a Italy had left the Axis in 1943 and joined the Allies. Thus she was not harshly treated, though she lost all her colonies. She also lost Trieste to Yugoslavia and had to pay reparations to Russia.

    b Austria was separated from Germany, and divided into military zones of occupation among the four Allies.

    c Czechoslovakia and Rumania lost some territory to Russia, but otherwise they, along with Hungary, Bulgaria, Albania and Greece kept their pre-war frontiers.

    d Finland, which had been on the Axis side, lost some territory to Russia, and agreed to lease the naval base of Porkkala to her.

C The United Nations Organisation

1 This was founded at a conference in San Francisco of Allied nations in April–June 1945. The UN Charter officially came into force on 24 October 1945, when it replaced the League of Nations. The Charter lays down the organisation of UNO, duties of member states, and defines its powers, which members agree to.

2 The General Assembly meets every year and has representatives from all member states, all such states having one vote each in the Assembly. The Assembly debates issues brought before it by members.

3 The Security Council carries out the Assembly's decisions, and sits continuously to deal with emergencies that may arise, e.g. an attack on a member state. Originally it had eleven members. Five (Britain, China, France, USA, USSR) were permanent, the other six were chosen for a period of two years from other member nations. The Council reaches decisions by a majority vote, but each of the permanent members has the right to veto any decision.

4 A headquarters for UNO was built in New York. There its work is supervised by its chief officer, the Secretary-General. The first man to hold the office was a Norwegian, Trygve Lie.

5 Many organisations carry out its work:

a at the end of the war, UNRRA (United Nations Relief and Rehabilitation Administration) organised supplies of food for liberated countries, where many were starving.

b UNESCO (United Nations Educational, Scientific and Cultural Organisation) devotes itself to world-wide education.

c WHO (World Health Organisation) fights disease, e.g. malaria.

d FAO (Food and Agriculture Organisation) aims to help poorer countries to increase their food supplies.

6 Some organisations were taken over from the old League of Nations:

a the Trusteeship Council took over the supervision of the former mandated colonies.

b the International Court of Justice still sits at The Hague in Holland.

c the International Telecommunication Union and the Universal Postal Union help co-operation on these matters.

Fig. 54 Post-war Europe.

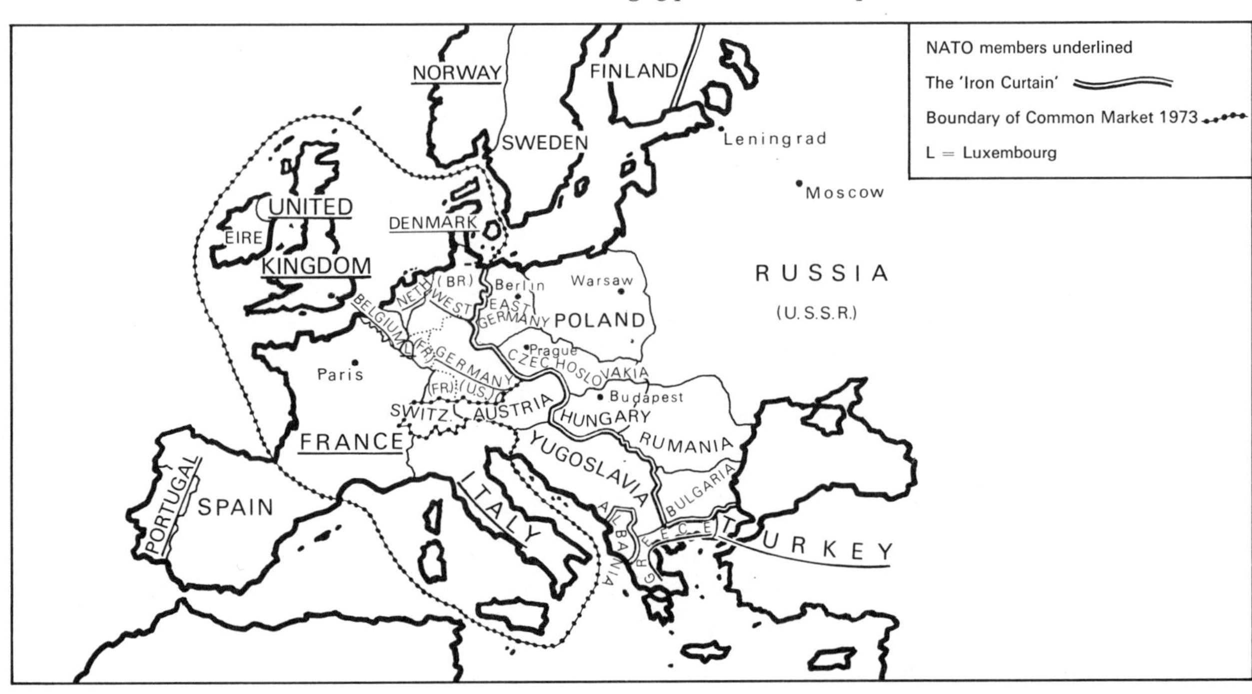

A The Cold War

Within a few months of the end of fighting in western Europe relations between Russia and the western powers were worsening rapidly. Soon, the situation was so tense that the phrase 'Cold War' came into use to describe the situation. This meant that Russia and the West were fighting each other, but without any actual shooting (which would have been a 'hot war').

Then, in a famous speech at Fulton, Missouri, in 1946, Churchill said: 'From Stettin on the Baltic to Trieste on the Adriatic, an Iron Curtain has descended across the continent'. It was soon clear that he was right.

1 In eastern Europe, Stalin used the presence of Russian armies to ensure the election of Communist governments. Yet force was not the only reason for the Communists' success. In many countries after the war the Russians were admired as liberators from Nazi tyranny.

Thus Poland, Czechoslovakia, Hungary, Rumania, Bulgaria and Albania all had Communist governments by the end of 1948. Opposition parties were broken up, and their leaders imprisoned or shot. The Church, especially the Roman Catholic Church, proved harder to crush. Though many of its leaders were imprisoned, e.g. Cardinal Mindzenty in Hungary, the Communists failed to break the power of the Church and later were forced to make agreed settlements on Church matters.

2 In Yugoslavia, which had been freed from the Germans more by its own efforts than by the Red Army, the Communist leader Tito stood up to Stalin, and asserted his country's independence of Moscow in economic and military matters. For instance, he did not force collective farming on the peasants as much as was favoured by Russia, and refused to enter an alliance with her. Instead he accepted economic aid from the West, especially the Americans.

3 Another set-back for Stalin came in Greece. At the end of the war Communist guerrillas (ELAS) tried to take over the country by force from the anti-Communist forces (EDES), but were stopped with British help. When the burden of aid to Greece became too much for Britain, the Americans stepped in and as a result ELAS was defeated.

4 Elections in western Europe produced no Communist governments:

a in France, de Gaulle formed a Coalition Government which included Communists, but he soon tired of the bickering and petty squabbles of party government, and resigned in 1946. He was succeeded by a rapid succession of shaky Coalition Ministries until his return to power in 1959.

b in Italy, the Communist Party was strong, but the Church was stronger. Thus the Catholic Christian Democratic Party has been the most important one in politics since the war, and its leaders have been members of all Italian governments.

5 The main threat to world peace seemed to be in Germany:

a the Allied Control Council, with American, British, French and Russian representatives, was set up at the end of the war to run the country, but worked badly due to friction between Russia and the other members.

b in 1948, by the London Agreement, the three western powers set up a single government for the whole of Western Germany. This led to the regrowth of party politics there, the two most important parties being the Christian Democrats, led then by Dr Adenauer, and the Social Democrats under Kurt Schumacher. The Russians set up a rival government for East Germany.

c then, in 1948, using a West German currency reform as an excuse for action, the Russians declared the whole of Berlin to be a part of East Germany. In June they closed all access by road, rail and canal from the west to Berlin, in an effort to force the western powers out of the city.

d the West replied by organising the famous Berlin Airlift (see fig. 55). In May 1949 the Russians backed down, and re-opened the routes to Berlin.

e one result of all this was the setting up of the two states of Germany in 1949. The German Federal Republic, or Western Germany, had its capital at Bonn, and the German Democratic Republic, or Eastern Germany, had its capital in the Russian sector of Berlin.

B Effects of the Cold War

President Truman and his advisers came to believe that Russia was the major threat to peace, and was bent on world domination. At the same time, the free countries of western Europe came together in an alliance to defend themselves with American help.

By the 'Truman Doctrine' the USA declared that Russia must not be allowed to advance any further, and promised to help maintain the independence of states threatened by a Communist take-over.

1 Under the 'Marshall Plan', named after the American Secretary of State George Marshall, the USA provided vast amounts of economic aid to western Europe e.g. money, raw materials and machinery. Russia refused this aid, and made her east European 'satellite' neighbours refuse it as well. Thus Marshall Aid helped to strengthen western Europe from the Communist threat from the east, while building up Europe to become a market for American goods. The OEEC (Organisation for European Economic Co-operation) was set up by the USA, Canada and the free countries of Europe to run the aid programme.

As a rival to Marshall Aid, Stalin drew up an economic plan for mutual aid in eastern Europe, called COMECON (Council for Mutual Economic Aid). However, Russia had been so devastated by the German invasion that she had little to offer for several years.

2 By the Treaty of Brussels, 1948, Britain, France and the Benelux countries (Belgium, the Netherlands and Luxembourg) formed an alliance against outside aggression. However, it was clear to many, especially the British Foreign Secretary Ernest Bevin, that western Europe could not defend itself against the might of Russia without American help.

3 Thus, in 1949, the North Atlantic Treaty Organisation (NATO) was formed:

a its members were the Brussels Treaty countries, the USA, Canada, Norway, Denmark, Iceland, Portugal, and Italy. Greece, Turkey and the German Federal Republic joined later. These countries agreed to join together to resist attack.

b NATO headquarters were set up at Fontainebleau, near Paris (called SHAPE, short for Supreme Headquarters Allied Powers in Europe). Its first Commander was General Eisenhower.

c all members agreed to provide a quota of armed forces on land, sea, and in the air. Equipment, such as guns and aircraft, was to be standardised as far as possible, and the forces of member countries trained together under each other's Commanders.

Yet it was clear that NATO's conventional (i.e. non-atomic weapon) forces would be no match for a Russian attack, and that all depended on American use of nuclear weapons to repel such an invasion if it came, especially after Russia announced that she had the atomic bomb in 1949.

d Russia attacked NATO as another example of American aggression, especially when Western Germany joined the alliance in 1955. This led Russia to form the Warsaw Treaty Organisation with the eastern European countries in 1955 (see page 67).

Fig. 55 The Berlin Airlift, 1948. Two million West Berliners had to be fed and kept warm for eleven months. At one stage aircraft from Britain, France and the USA were landing every five minutes, loaded with supplies. Even so, there was strict food and fuel rationing. The airlift went on night and day in all weathers, and cost the lives of over fifty aircrew.

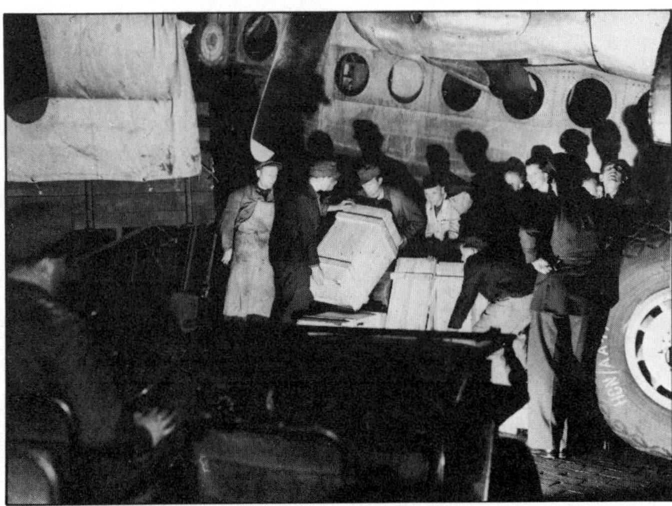

C Khrushchev and the 'Thaw'

In March 1953 Stalin died. Nikita Khrushchev emerged successful from the rivals for succession to Stalin's position in Russia, and under him great changes were carried out both inside Russia and in her relations with other countries.

1 Although there were to be times when relations between Russia and the west, especially the USA, were to be strained, and indeed it seemed for a few days as if an atomic war was to break out over the Cuban Crisis in 1962 (see page 69) there was an overall improvement in relations between east and west under Khrushchev.

This improvement has come to be called the 'Thaw'. Khrushchev himself put it into words when he said that although the Communist east and Capitalist west must compete, it was possible for them to do so without fighting, following a policy of 'peaceful co-existence'. Of course, he said that Communism must eventually triumph, but would do so without a world war.

2 Khrushchev's reasons for this change in policy were probably that many Russians realised the folly of atomic war, and that Russia would benefit from increased trade with the west (in the seventies she was to import huge amounts of grain from the USA).

She could also then reduce the size and cost of her vast armed forces, and use the savings to improve the standard of living of the Russian people.

Fig. 56 Nikita Khrushchev (1894-1971)

He must have realised that the west had no intention of attacking Russia, and many of Russia's leaders came to believe that the main threat to their country in future would come from China (see Ch. 9).

3 However, he had to be careful not to change Russian policies too quickly. There were still many 'Stalinists' in positions of power in Russia and in her eastern European satellites, who wanted to stick to the old policies.

Leaders of Russia's armed forces opposed any reductions in their size. Also, Russians had never forgotten the terrible sufferings of their country from the German invasion in World War Two, and were determined that nothing like it should happen again. Thus any relaxation of Russia's tight hold over her satellites in Europe was to be prevented.

Of course, much of the struggle that went on in Russia behind the scenes over her foreign policies is not known to the west, and many of the reasons for Khrushchev's actions must be guesswork. Yet the sudden changes in his attitude that sometimes took place may have been caused by a need to quieten powerful opposition in Russia.

4 From 1953 to 1961 Eisenhower was the President of the USA, and tended to leave foreign affairs in the hands of his Secretary of State, John Foster Dulles, who distrusted the Russians and failed to respond to Khrushchev's 'peace offensive'. The American Central Intelligence Agency (CIA) continued to encourage plots to overthrow Communist régimes in eastern Europe and in Cuba.

D Eastern Europe, 1953–6

In 1953 there were strikes and riots in East Berlin, which started as a dispute over the wages paid to building workers. Russian tanks had to be called in to restore order, and many civilians were killed.

1 Yet in Czechoslovakia, Hungary and Poland popular demand brought changes:

    a in general many political prisoners were released, such as Communists and Socialists who had opposed the policies of Stalin and his followers.

b the powers of the secret police were reduced, and censorship of press and radio relaxed somewhat.

c in economic affairs the Stalinist 'line' had always been that in agriculture farming must be collective, while industrially the stress must be on production of capital goods, e.g. machinery, rather than consumer goods such as clothing and domestic appliances. Now, in eastern Europe, as in Russia itself, there was more emphasis on production of consumer goods and a slowing down of collectivisation of farming. Also, Russia began to interfere less in the internal economic policies of these countries.

d yet Russia would not allow reform to go too far. In all her satellites, the Communist Party remained firmly in control, and in 1955 the Warsaw Pact was drawn up as a rival to NATO.

2 The Hungarian Rising, 1956. The fact that Russia would not allow her east European neighbours too much independence was clearly shown in Hungary:

a here, Rákosi, a Stalinist, had been replaced as Premier by the moderate Imre Nagy. In Hungary, as in Poland, there was strong, traditional anti-Russian feeling. This, and the fact that relaxation of censorship allowed people to voice criticism more freely, coupled with a bad harvest in 1956, led to riots of students and armed workers in Budapest, the capital, in October.

b the rioters demanded further reform, e.g. abolition of the secret police, and evacuation of Hungary by Russian forces. Nagy promised to meet these demands, hold free elections, and in effect take Hungary out of the Soviet bloc.

c for a few days the Russian troops left the country, but invaded in force in early November. The Hungarians put up a brave resistance in the streets of Budapest, and inflicted heavy losses on the Russian tanks. Over 25 000 Hungarians were reported killed, but the end was certain.

d Hungarian resistance was crushed. Nagy was shot by the Russians and a pro-Russian government was formed under János Kádár.

About 200 000 Hungarian refugees fled to the west.

3 The free world, and many west European Communist Parties, condemned Russia's action, but could not intervene with force, as this would have led to a world war. Fortunately for Russia, the Suez crisis diverted much of the world's attention from Hungarian affairs at the time.

4 The crushing of the Hungarian rising made it clear that Russia could not allow her Communist neighbours to break ranks with her (as was also shown in Czechoslovakia in 1967–8). If Hungary had been allowed independence, other satellite states would almost certainly have followed.

5 About this time (see Ch. 9) Russia started to increase her influence in the Middle East. In general, she supported the Arab cause, while the west, especially the USA, supported Israel.

Fig. 57 A wrecked Russian tank and lorry against a shell-torn background – Budapest during the Hungarian rising of 1956.

E Russia and China

During the civil war in China after World War Two (see page 76), Russia had helped the Communists with arms and equipment. When the Communists won, Russia gave China economic aid and sent many experts to help to develop China's industries. After about 1956 relations between Russia and China began to worsen.

1 Traditionally, Russia had always feared that China's countless millions, when properly organised and led, would seek to expand into Russia's vast and thinly-populated Asian provinces.

China's leaders began to feel that Russia was betraying the true spirit of Communism, in such matters as belief in peaceful co-existence with the west, slowing down of collectivisation of agriculture, increased output of consumer goods by industry, and the more liberal outlook in Russia generally since Stalin's death.

2 Russia stopped economic aid to China and withdrew all her expert advisers. Border disputes between the two countries became frequent, and led to local fighting between the two armies. In 1962 Russia supported India over her dispute with China (see Ch. 9). Then, Russia's fears were increased when in 1964 China exploded an atomic bomb, and thus became a nuclear power. In the late 1960s Khrushchev's successors, such as Kosygin, were openly denouncing China as the enemy.

China secured little support among other Communist countries. Only tiny Albania followed her lead, and denounced Russia.

F Russia and Germany

The problem of how and when to reunify Germany continued to cause ill-feeling between Russia and the west.

1 In 1954 the four powers occupying Germany (Britain, France, Russia and the USA) met in Berlin to try to achieve a settlement over Germany. This would have meant the reunification of West and East Germany and the setting up of a new German state. (Earlier, the four powers had evacuated Austria, which became a neutral state.)

The talks broke down, however, and led to Germany becoming more firmly divided than ever. The west now recognised West Germany as an independent state, the German Federal Republic which was admitted to NATO. This led (see page 67) to the signing of the Warsaw Pact, yet in the same year Russia recognised the Federal Republic, as the west had done. Russia hoped in vain that the west would recognise Eastern Germany (the German Democratic Republic) in return.

2 Russia feared that a free, reunited Germany would be a possible threat to her security. To many in the west this seemed most unlikely, yet Russia had suffered two German invasions in the twentieth century.

In 1958 Khrushchev suddenly demanded that the Allies withdraw from West Berlin by May 1959. However, when the deadline came, he took no action. Instead, he paid a visit to the USA and had talks with President Eisenhower. There, at Camp David, the American and Russian leaders agreed to meet the following year in a summit conference in Paris. It was hoped to reach a settlement on the German problem, which both sides recognised as a threat to world peace, and on disarmament, particularly nuclear weapons.

G Paris and the U2 Incident, 1960

People the world over had high hopes of the Paris Summit Conference. Apart from Eisenhower and Khrushchev, the French and British leaders, de Gaulle and Macmillan, were present. Yet nothing was achieved.

1 Shortly before the conference started, the Russians shot down a remarkable American reconnaissance plane, the U2, which was on a flight from an American base in Pakistan across Russia. Its pilot, Gary Powers, had orders to photograph Russian bases.

2 This sensational incident may have caused such strong feelings among Russia's leaders that Khrushchev had no choice but to call off his 'peace offensive'. In Paris, he accused the USA of trickery by appearing to support a peace conference while flying warplanes over Russia, and demanded that those responsible be punished, and that such flights must be stopped.

3 Eisenhower would not agree to all of Khrushchev's demands, and said that the U2 flights were purely defensive, to give warning of a surprise Russian attack. Khrushchev then left Paris, and the conference collapsed.

H The Vienna Conference, 1961

In June 1961 the new American President, John F. Kennedy, met Khrushchev in Vienna to try to reach a settlement. Once again nothing was achieved, either on Germany or on wider issues.

1 As a result, the East Germans built a formidable wall across Berlin, along the boundary between the western and eastern sectors of the city. They were forced to do this to check the flood of emigrants from East to West Germany, where the standard of living was much higher.

2 West Berliners and West Germans resented this strongly, but America and the western powers in general recognised that East Germany had been forced to build the wall to stop the drain on her population, rather than as an attempt to cause friction.

3 In the 1970s, the German Social Democratic Party came to power in Western Germany for the first time, led by the former mayor of West Berlin, Willy Brandt. He helped, by personal visits, to improve relations with East Germany and Poland.

West Germany signed a treaty recognising the Oder-Neisse frontier between East Germany and Poland, while in 1973 both East and West Germany were admitted to UNO.

I The Cuban Crisis

This, the most serious crisis yet between America and Russia, came in October 1962.

1 The USA was traditionally pledged, by the 'Monroe Doctrine', to resist any growth of overseas control in any part of the American continent. In addition, Americans had large investments in Cuba, e.g. in sugar plantations.

Therefore when the Communist Fidel Castro, having overthrown the brutal dictatorship of Batista in 1959, went on to take over the country and some American property, many Americans were outraged.

Fig. 58   The American U2 spy plane.

Fig. 59   The Berlin Wall, 1962.

2 The USA refused to buy Cuban sugar, and introduced a trade embargo. This meant, for instance, that Cuba could not buy any motor vehicles from the USA, or even spares for the ones she had bought in the past.

Khrushchev saw a chance to extend Russian influence, and went on to offer Castro financial aid as well as a trade treaty and the services of technical experts.

3 In 1961 Kennedy reacted by supporting a badly-planned attempt by anti-Castro exiles to land in Cuba at the Bay of Pigs, and to start a rebellion aimed at Castro's overthrow. Though this attempt was a fiasco, the USA continued to harbour the exiles in Florida, and the CIA encouraged further anti-Castro schemes.

4 Then in October 1962 the crisis worsened and almost led to nuclear war. President Kennedy announced that American reconnaissance planes had spotted in Cuba several sites for launching Soviet-built missiles, capable of delivering a nuclear attack on the United States.

Some of his advisers wanted an all-out attack on Cuba, but Kennedy kept his head, and instead

told the world that Russia must dismantle the sites and take away the missiles. Until the Russians agreed to this, the American Fleet would 'quarantine' (blockade) Cuba to prevent any further Russian ships from reaching the island.

5 For a few days the world held its breath. Khrushchev said that Russian ships on their way to Cuba would force their way through the American 'quarantine'. US forces all over the world prepared for atomic war.

Then Khrushchev gave way and ordered his ships to reverse course. Soon the American and Russian leaders were in touch by telephone and a settlement was reached. Kennedy agreed not to encourage steps to overthrow Castro, while Khrushchev agreed to dismantle and remove the missiles.

6 There was general admiration in the west for Kennedy's calm handling of the crisis, but some of the Russian leaders felt that Khrushchev had gone too far in taking such a frightful risk. This was one of the reasons given by the Russians for Khrushchev's downfall in 1964 (see Ch. 11). He was succeeded by two men, Brehznev and Kosygin.

Fig. 60   Russian forces in Prague, Czechoslovakia, 1968.

7 Two good things came out of the Cuban affair:

a both sides agreed to install a special direct telephone link between the White House, the President's official residence in Washington, and the Kremlin, seat of Russia's Government. This 'hot line' could be used to put the two leaders in touch at a few seconds' notice in case of a future crisis.

b also, the USA, Russia and Britain signed a nuclear test ban treaty, agreeing not to carry out any more nuclear tests in the atmosphere.

This was a big step forward for world health as well as for peace. Nuclear explosions in the atmosphere lead to 'fall-out' or scattering of radioactive dust, which can remain dangerous for many years. The fall-out finds its way through the air and rain into plants and animals which in turn are eaten by people, who can develop fatal diseases, e.g. leukaemia (blood cancer), as a result.

J Czechoslovakia, 1968–70

1 Here the events of Hungary in 1956 were repeated. In the face of growing demands for more personal freedom and more consumer goods in a freer economy, the 'hard-line' President, Novotny, was forced to resign, and was replaced as President by General Svoboda, who was supported by Alex Dubchek, First Secretary of the Czech Communist Party.

2 The new régime introduced sweeping reforms:

a the powers of the secret police were reduced, and censorship abolished.

b many political prisoners were released.

c factories and shops were to have more freedom to make and sell what they wished, without state control.

d trade with western countries was to be developed, and travel to them permitted.

e Parliament was to have more control over the government, and parties other than the Communists allowed some say in public affairs.

3 As in Hungary earlier, Russia's leaders decided that the reformers were going too far, and threatening Russia's security. In August 1968,

Warsaw Pact armies, mostly Russian, invaded Czechoslovakia. Dubchek was arrested, but later released and given the minor post of Ambassador to Turkey.

Though realising that it was useless to try to stop the Russians by armed force (the Czech army was ordered not to resist the invasion) the Czech people showed by demonstrations and riots that they were bitterly opposed to the occupation of their country.

4 Eventually Russia was able to force a pro-Russian and less reforming government on the Czechs, led by Dr Husak, but the Czech crisis caused great hostility to Russia in the west, where many Communist parties went so far as to openly condemn the Russian action.

K Nuclear Weapons

The Czech affair made improvement in the relations between east and west impossible for a while, as did events in Vietnam (see Ch. 9).

1 However, both the USA and Russia were realising by the early seventies that both sides would benefit from a halt in the nuclear arms race and in the colossal spending by both sides on increasingly complicated and costly anti-missile defence systems.

2 Since 1945 both countries have spent enormous amounts on rocket bases, atomic missiles and warships (including submarines) equipped to fire nuclear warheads. However, talks on a strategic arms limitation treaty (SALT) began in 1970.

L The 'Third World'

This consists mainly of countries in Africa and Asia, which were once under colonial rule e.g. India and the Congo.

1 Such countries have the name 'Third World' because they are allied to neither east nor west, but hope to remain neutral, and if possible to receive aid from both sides.

2 They share many desperate problems, such as a very low standard of living for their people, rapidly-growing populations that outstrip food supplies, lack of money to develop their resources, and lack of schools and doctors.

3 Such countries have a large bloc of votes in total at UNO, and use their influence to further good relations between east and west.

A The 'Palestine Problem' to 1945

1 In 1917, to secure Jewish support during the First World War, Britain promised, by the 'Balfour Declaration', that she would support the setting-up in Palestine of a 'national home for the Jewish people'. At the time Palestine was, and had been for centuries, occupied by the Turks as part of the Ottoman Empire, and had a mixed population of Arabs and Jews.

2 With Turkey's defeat in 1918, Palestine and much of the Ottoman Empire was mandated to Britain at the Peace Settlement.

However, the Arabs made it clear that they were strongly opposed to the idea of a Jewish state in Palestine. What, they said, would happen to all the Arabs there?

The Jews said there would be room for both races, but bitter hatred between them has in fact made a settlement of the problem impossible.

3 In the years between the two World Wars, Jews from overseas came and settled in Palestine, especially when Hitler started his persecution of them in Germany. The Arabs felt that Jews were taking over Palestine, and riots and bloodshed between the two races took place. Britain sent troops to restore order and tried to restrict the flow of Jewish immigrants.

B The Birth of Israel

1 After the end of the Second World War in 1945, the flow of Jewish immigrants was resumed, and Britain was accused by both Jews and Arabs of favouring the other side. For instance, Jewish gangs such as Haganah and the Stern Gang attacked both British and Arabs.

2 In Britain, Attlee's Labour Government decided to pull out of Palestine altogether and leave the problem to the United Nations.

In November 1947 the UN decided, to the Jews' delight, to partition Palestine. This decision the Arabs would not accept, as it meant setting up a Jewish state.

3 As soon as the British pulled out in 1948, the Jews proclaimed the new state of Israel, with Dr Weizmann as President and David Ben-Gurion as Prime Minister:

a war with the surrounding Arab countries, who had formed themselves into an 'Arab League' followed. To the surprise of many, Israel defeated the Arabs, who had to agree to a truce arranged by the UN in 1949.

Fig. 61   The Middle East since 1945.

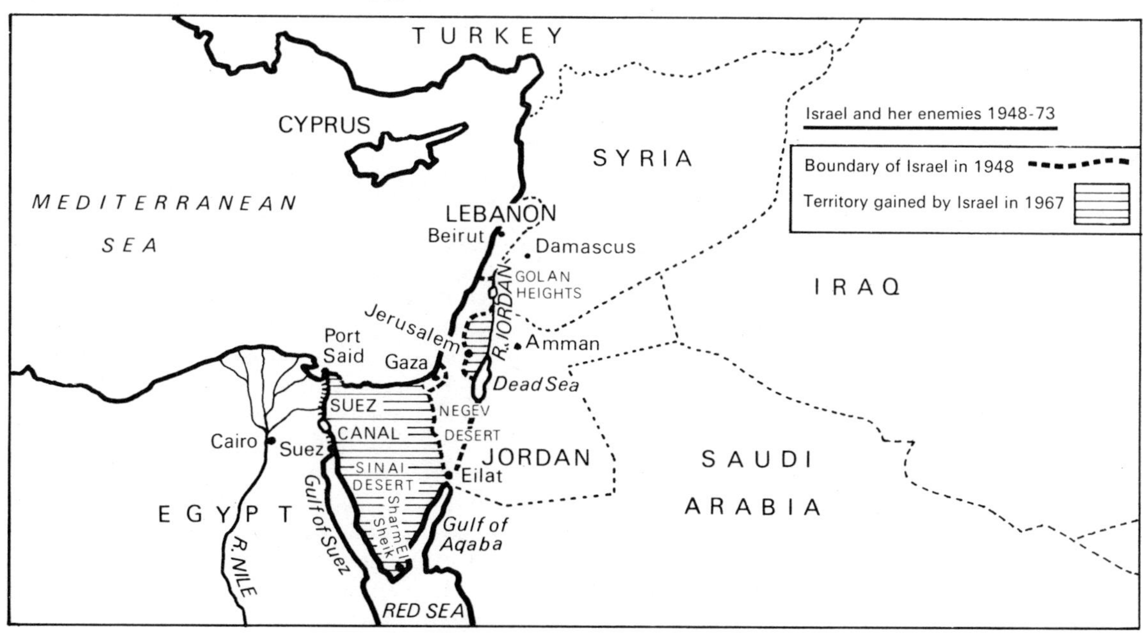

b the Arabs refused however, and have continued to refuse, to recognise the state of Israel.

c also, almost 700 000 Arabs were driven from their homes in Israel by the war. They and their descendants still live in refugee camps and long to overthrow Israel so that they can return home.

d thus it is not surprising that conflict between Arab and Jew has exploded into full-scale war on three occasions since.

C The New Egypt

1 Britain had occupied and virtually run Egypt since 1882, partly because of the importance to Britain's Empire, and later to her oil supplies, of the Suez Canal. By 1955 however, Britain had pulled out of Egypt, including the Canal Zone, as the strip of land on either side of the Suez Canal was called.

In July 1952 a group of army officers, led by General Neguib and Colonel Nasser, who had been sickened by the corruption and inefficiency of King Farouk's régime (which they blamed for Egypt's poor showing against Israel in 1948–9) led a revolution. Farouk was deposed, and later a Republic of Egypt was proclaimed.

2 Nasser took over leadership of Egypt from Neguib in 1954, and introduced many much-needed reforms:

a land was given to the desperately poor fellahin (peasants).

b new industries were encouraged.

c plans were made to build a huge new dam at Aswan which would provide electricity, help to irrigate much more land, and control the often wasteful floods of the Nile.

3 Not content with domestic reform, however, Nasser was determined that Egypt should lead the Arab world:

a to do this he made alliances with other Arab countries, built up Egypt's forces (buying arms from Iron Curtain countries, especially Russia), and in speeches and other propaganda voiced his hatred of Israel.

b at the same time he harboured guerrillas who raided Israel.

c he also helped rebels in Algeria against French rule.

D Suez

1 Nasser's policies led the USA and Britain to try to bring him to heel by withdrawing an offer they had made to help finance the building of the Aswan Dam. The Suez Canal was owned by an international company, whose shares were mainly held in Britain and France.

Nasser determined to use the canal's income to pay for the Aswan Dam, so in July 1956 he announced that Egypt was nationalising the canal. His promise of compensation did not satisfy the British and French governments. To Sir Anthony Eden, who had become Prime Minister in place of Churchill in 1954, he was a dictator like Hitler. Like Hitler, he must be overthrown. The French agreed.

2 Though it was denied at the time, Britain, France and Israel met secretly and agreed on a joint attack on Egypt. In late October 1956 Israeli forces attacked across the Sinai Desert and in a few days had routed the Egyptian forces. Britain and France issued an 'ultimatum' to both sides to stop fighting and withdraw to ten miles on either side of the Suez Canal. Israel accepted but Egypt refused. Nasser appealed to the UN Security Council, which summoned a special meeting.

3 Meanwhile French and British amphibious forces were landed, supported by paratroops. They succeeded in seizing the canal, but not before the Egyptians had blocked it by sinking ships along its length.

However, almost every other country in the world, including the USA and the USSR, condemned the British and French action and voted against it in a debate at UNO headquarters. America threatened to withdraw monetary support from Britain unless she withdrew, and Russia threatened direct intervention.

4 Thus there was nothing Britain and France could do but to agree to a cease-fire, and to hand over their positions along the canal to a UN Force, which was to patrol the border between Egypt and Israel to keep the two enemies apart. Thus, Israel had defeated Egypt, but gained little (apart from the Gaza strip) from the struggle.

The Suez affair was a big blow to British and French prestige, and marked the last attempt by either power to use force on a weaker country. Britain's position in the Middle East was undermined. Jordan now looked up to Egypt rather than to Britain.

5 Nasser's prestige was now at its height, and Russia had a firm footing in the Middle East, where she was to give strong support to the Arabs against the Israelis.

E The 'Six-Day War', 1967

1 Nasser was able to unite almost the whole Arab world in support of his plans to crush Israel. There were differences among the Arabs, e.g. hostility between Nasser and King Hussein of Jordan, but the Arabs were united in hatred of the Jews.

In 1967 Nasser increased the pressure on Israel. He ordered the UN peacekeeping force, which had stood between the Egyptians and the Israelis in Sinai since 1956, to leave. This they did. Then Egyptian forces occupied Sharm el Sheik on the Straits of Tiran at the entrance to the Gulf of Aqaba, and Nasser declared the Straits closed to Israeli shipping. As the Suez Canal was already closed to the Israelis, this was a serious blow.

2 By now Nasser had enlarged and re-equipped his forces with Russian weapons. The west, especially the USA and France, supplied Israel. Nasser was confident that the time had come to crush Israel.

However, on 5 June, the Israelis struck first, without warning. Much of Nasser's air force, and those of Jordan and Syria, were wiped out on the ground by the Israelis' French-built Mystere and Mirage fighter-bombers. Soon the remaining Arab aircraft had been shot from the skies.

3 This left the Arab land forces wide open to air attack. In Sinai the Egyptian Army was beaten within two days. The Jordanian Army was defeated and driven back across the Jordan. Then Israel switched her forces north to defeat the Syrians in the Golan Heights.

Thus within six days the war was over. Nasser and his allies had suffered a crushing defeat, and were forced to ask for a cease-fire. This Israel agreed to, though she kept most of the land she had conquered (see fig. 61).

F The 'Yom Kippur War', 1973

1 Nasser died in 1970, but his successor, Sadat, kept to the same policy regarding Israel. The Arab countries would not recognise her, nor would they make peace until Israel agreed to give up her conquests.

The Six-Day War had increased the number of Arab refugees, and their organisations such as the Palestine Liberation Organisation (PLO) continued to harass Israel by raids on Israel's territory from bases in Arab countries. They also carried out a policy of 'skyjacking', hijacking airliners in flight to draw attention to their cause. Other activities included planting bombs in Jewish-owned stores and posting letter-bombs to prominent Jews. Arab 'freedom fighters' or 'terrorists' (the name depends on where one's sympathies lie) killed several Israeli competitors at the Olympic Games in Munich in 1972.

2 In general, the west supported Israel, but many westerners were also sympathetic to the Arab refugees in their hopeless position – living in squalid camps, with no future prospects and nothing to do but brood on revenge.

3 Full-scale war broke out again on 6 October 1973, the Jewish Day of Atonement (Yom Kippur). Arab forces attacked, and this time Israel was almost caught napping.

Her armies came close to defeat in Sinai, where the Egyptians crossed the Suez Canal and breached the Israeli Bar Lev defence line. However, in a daring manoeuvre, the Israeli Army crossed the canal to the west bank and cut off most of the main Egyptian Army. To the north the Golan Heights saw bitter fighting before the Syrians were defeated.

Once again the UN arranged a cease-fire and a partial settlement was reached at Geneva in 1975.

G The Oil Problem

In 1973 the Arabs, realising the powerful hold their position as major oil producers gave them over the west, decided to put this weapon to use.

1 They declared, for a time, a ban on oil supplies to countries such as the USA which they accused of being pro-Israeli, and a reduction of supplies to others. Oil-producing countries,

Arab and non-Arab, were members of OPEC (an organisation of Oil Producing and Exporting Countries). This decided on a massive increase in oil prices, which countries such as Britain had to pay.

2 These actions did not in fact help the Arabs much in their fight against Israel, but they caused serious problems to people in Britain and throughout the world.

H China Between the World Wars

1 China had been an Empire for centuries until a Republic was founded in 1911 by Sun Yat Sen, leader of the Kuomintang (Nationalist) Party. Though a huge country, with a vast and industrious population, China was in fact weak. Her agriculture was backward, with most of the peasants toiling hard to pay rents to greedy landlords. Few people could read or write. Her industries and railways were few. Her neighbours, such as Japan and Russia, were greedy, while China's Army was weak and the Navy almost non-existent.

2 She was further weakened by constant civil war, waged by powerful war-lords and their followers. The central government was usually unable to stop them. Yet China was, as Napoleon called her, a 'sleeping giant'. He saw that, given firm government and proper development of her resources, China could be a great power.

3 When Sun Yat Sen died in 1925 he was succeeded by Chiang-Kai-Shek, who ruled more as a dictator. By the late twenties Chiang-Kai-Shek had put an end to much of the disorder inside China.

However, he faced a rival in the Communist Mao Tse-Tung, with whom he quarrelled and fought. At the time it seemed as if the Communists might be crushed by Chiang's armies, which conquered a Soviet Republic set up in Hunan by Mao's followers.

4 This led the Communists to undertake the famous 'long march' of 6 000 miles, from October 1934 to October 1935. 100 000 of them, led by Mao, determined to march from Hunan to a remote area of Shensi, where they hoped they would be safe. Despite attacks by Nationalist troops and losses from cold and starvation, about 20 000 survived the march.

5 Then what the Japanese called the 'China

Fig. 62 Mass rally in Communist China.

Incident' started in 1937 (see Ch. 3). China was too weak to resist Japan's attack. At first, all Chiang-Kai-Shek could do was to retreat into the interior of his vast country, and move his capital from Peking to Chunking. China was saved by the entry of the USA into the war in 1941, which led to Japan's defeat in 1945.

I The Communist Takeover

1 With Japan's defeat a full-scale civil war broke out between the Nationalists and the Communists, spreading from the north to involve the whole country. The Americans were anxious to stop China from going Communist and so supplied Chiang's forces lavishly with military equipment and financial aid.

2 Yet the Kuomintang were forced to retreat everywhere. The Communists won popular support by branding Chiang as the tool of China's landlords and capitalists, as well as being the lackey of the American imperialists.

Chiang's dictatorship lost the support of the masses, especially when the Communists promised to distribute land among the peasants. Much of the Nationalist régime was corrupt and inefficient, so that American money was pocketed by Chiang's followers, instead of being used to fight the Communists, while the arms America sent were often traded to them.

3 Thus by 1949 Chiang-Kai-Shek's Nationalist followers had been forced out of the mainland of China altogether, and held only Formosa and a few small offshore islands.

On 1 October 1949, the People's Republic of China was proclaimed by the victorious Communists, with Mao Tse-Tung as its leader.

4 Chairman Mao's new People's Republic faced grave problems:

a years of fighting against the Japanese, and the civil war, had caused great destruction.

b food was scarce.

c many factories had been damaged or destroyed.

d communications were bad as many railways and roads had been damaged or neglected for years.

e prices were sky-high.

5 As in Russia after the Revolution, the Communist Government of China acted with great vigour:

a most factories, companies, newspapers and banks were taken over by the state. The media (press and radio) were especially subject to strict control, and poured out a stream of government propaganda.

b the land was distributed among the peasants.

c opponents of the régime were ruthlessly dealt with.

d Chinese people, of all ages, were forced to study and learn the 'party line' on all matters.

6 Also as in Russia, Mao drew up Five Year Plans for the country's progress, the first starting in 1952, the second – the 'Great Leap Forward' – in 1957. On the land, as in industry, high targets for production were set, but not always reached.

In the countryside, the peasants' land was grouped into collective farms, and they were to share equipment and tools. Food production rose, but natural disasters such as floods and drought led to famine in 1961, and meant that China had to import grain from the capitalist world.

In industry much progress was made. The stress was on heavy industry, e.g. machinery, and the building of steel works and power stations, rather than on producing consumer goods.

7 China must have found it hard, while trying to achieve the goals of her Five Year Plans, to afford to quarrel with Russia and to interfere in other countries' affairs.

Russia stopped aid to China, and withdrew her technical advisers. At the same time, China maintained huge armed forces, and, in the fifties and sixties, fought in the Korean War, invaded Tibet and attacked India (in a brief border war in the Himalayas in 1962) as well as supplying the Communists in Vietnam with arms.

8 One reason for China's quarrel with Russia was the feeling that Russia was betraying the ideals of Communism by adopting a more liberal internal policy and following the policy of 'peaceful co-existence' with western countries. To ensure that China kept to what he considered the path of true Communism, Mao Tse-

Tung launched the 'Cultural Revolution' of the mid-sixties.

9 Large numbers of young people, called 'Red Guards', marched about China and demonstrated in favour of Mao's ideas, which were summed up in a little red book, 'The Thoughts of Chairman Mao'. They stressed the need for hard work, and the virtues of a simple life without luxuries, sharing with others, and physical fitness. At the same time, western ideas in dress and music were attacked.

Foreigners were puzzled as to what was going on in China, especially as few foreign correspondents were allowed into the country, and those who were allowed in were closely watched.

10 In the early seventies, despite their support for opposite sides in the Vietnam war, there were signs of lessening tension between China and the USA. America had always opposed Communist China's entry into the United Nations, and supported Nationalist China's claim to sit there instead. In 1971, however, the USA did not oppose Communist China's admission to UN and the expulsion of the Nationalists. Then in 1972 President Nixon made a much-publicised and successful visit to China. By this time China had developed her own hydrogen bomb, and was thus a world power.

J The Korean War

1 Background:

a Korea had been ruled by Japan since 1910, until her defeat in 1945. Then American forces occupied South Korea while the Russians occupied the north. The two armies had the 38th parallel of latitude as a boundary between them. This was supposed to be a temporary arrangement until a government was set up for the whole of Korea.

However, as the cold war developed, this proved impossible to carry out. Instead, the Russians set up a Communist Government in the north under Kim Il-Sung (The People's Democratic Republic), while in the south the Americans supported the government of Syngman Rhee.

b however, both Russia and the USA withdrew their forces from Korea by mid-1949. This was an advantage to the Communists, as North Korea was more industrialised and prosperous than the south.

2 The fighting:

a after various border incidents, North Korean troops crossed the 38th parallel and invaded South Korea in June 1950. The USA acted quickly, and sent forces from Japan to help the South Koreans.

At the time, Russia was boycotting meetings of the United Nations, so that they were unable to veto a UN resolution to help South Korea defend herself.

b as a result, although most of the forces sent to help South Korea were American, other countries, such as Britain and Turkey, sent contingents. While help was on its way, the South Korean forces were driven back to a corner of their country around Pusan. Then the UN forces, commanded by the American General MacArthur, drove the Communists back.

Fig. 63   The Korean War, 1950-3.

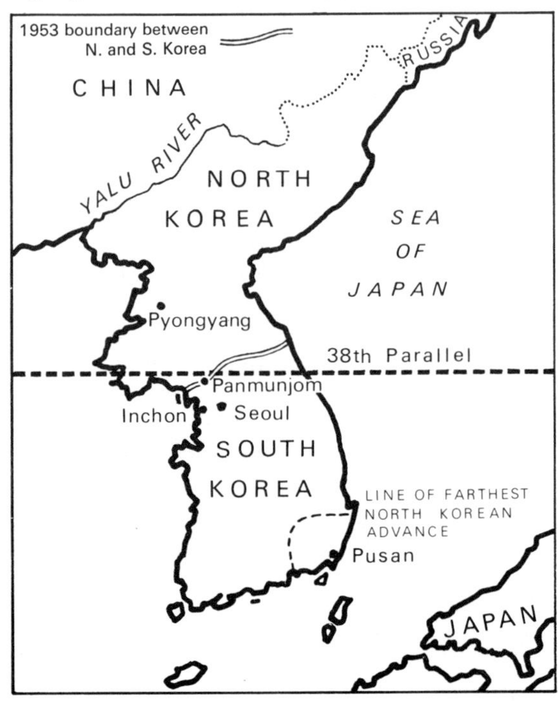

c after a daring and successful landing at Inchon, the UN forces recaptured the South Korean capital, Seoul, and advanced into North Korea.

Then China intervened, fearing that the UN forces might advance to her border with Korea on the Yalu River, and even cross it. She did not actually declare war, but sent hundreds of thousands of 'volunteer' soldiers to help the North Koreans. They attacked in October, and drove the UN armies back across the 38th parallel before their advance was stopped.

d now a serious threat to world peace developed. MacArthur, a brilliant soldier with an intense hatred of Communism, wanted to bomb Chinese factories and power stations in Manchuria, and even use the atomic bomb against them. Such action would almost certainly have led to all-out war with Russia entering on China's side (they were still good friends at that time). Therefore President Truman dismissed MacArthur.

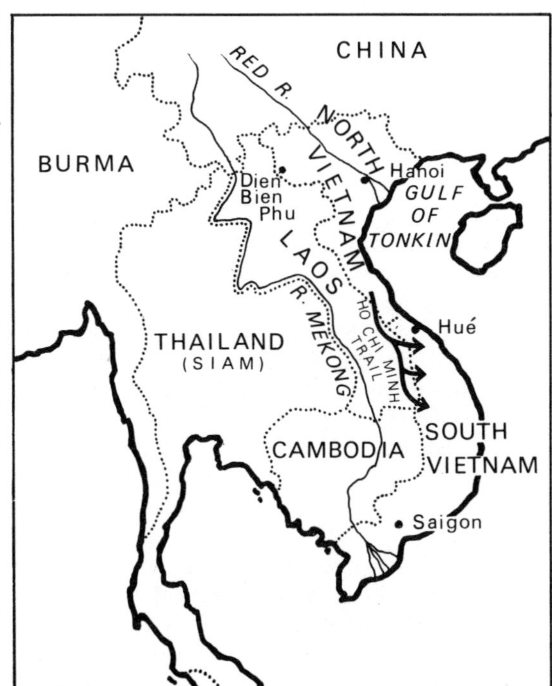

Fig. 64 Indo-China (later Vietnam) since 1945.

3 The end of the war:

a by now both sides were tiring of the war, which had caused great destruction in Korea. Peace talks were begun at Kaisong in 1951, but it was two years before an armistice was signed (July 1953). A truce commission was set up and meets regularly at Panmunjom, to settle disputes between North and South Korea.

b the war had awakened America and the west to the power of the new China. The United Nations had acted effectively, but only because of Russia's absence. In the USA itself, the war helped the rise of 'McCarthyism' (see Ch. 10).

K Vietnam

1 France in Vietnam:

a before the Second World War, Vietnam, Laos and Cambodia formed the French colony of Indo-China. During the war it was occupied by the Japanese. They were resisted by the Communist Vietminh forces, led by Ho Chi Minh and Vo Nguyen Giap, who held much of the north of the country by the time the war ended in 1945.

b after Japan's defeat, France reoccupied the south, and then set out to reconquer the north from the Communists. The USA helped the French with weapons and equipment, but not troops. They found it impossible to defeat the Communist guerrillas.

c therefore the French planned, in 1954, to tempt the Communists into a large-scale pitched battle, which the French believed they must win, as the Communists were believed to have no heavy guns and in any case would be unable to supply a large army for long. Yet it was the French who were beaten, at Dien Bien Phu. General Giap's forces, supplied by tens of thousands of peasants, proved too strong for the French, and had heavy artillery after all.

d France decided that Indo-China was not worth the effort involved. Therefore a peace conference met at Geneva in July 1954, where, as well as France and the governments of North and South Vietnam, Britain, China, the USA and the USSR were represented.

2 The Geneva Settlement stated that Laos and Cambodia should be independent states, and that Vietnam should be partitioned temporarily along the line of the 17th parallel of latitude. Within two years free elections were to be held for the whole of Vietnam, and the two halves of the country reunited.

Yet the USA and South Vietnam refused to sign this agreement, and thus nothing was really settled.

3 Further conflict:

a in the south, the government of Ngo Dinh Diem refused to allow free elections, which would probably have resulted in a Communist victory in Vietnam as a whole. His régime was weak and corrupt, but bolstered up by the Americans, who stepped into Vietnamese affairs as France bowed out of them. The American Secretary of State, Dulles, was determined to stop any further spread of Communism, and later Presidents Kennedy and Johnson followed a similar policy.

b among the peasantry in the south, there was much support for the Vietcong, as the Vietminh Communists now called themselves, and following Diem's assassination in 1963 the Vietcong stepped up their guerrilla campaign in South Vietnam. They were supplied from the north and from China along the 'Ho Chi Minh Trail' through Laos.

c the United States then became increasingly involved in the fighting. Opinion in America and throughout the free world was divided. America's supporters said that the Vietcong secured support in the south through terror methods, that they were seeking to undermine a free state, and that South Vietnam was a bastion in the struggle against Communism. Many held to the belief that if South Vietnam fell to the Communists, so would the whole of south-east Asia.

Supporters of American withdrawal from Vietnam, on the other hand, said that the mass of the people there supported the Communists, and that the USA was supporting a corrupt dictatorship against the wishes of the Vietnamese people.

d at first, the US sent equipment to the south, and advisers on its use. Troops were sent to guard the supply depots, then to attack the Vietcong. Using an attack on an American destroyer in the Gulf of Tonkin as an excuse, the US began air raids on the north, which soon became heavy. By 1967 America had 400 000 troops in Vietnam, yet the Vietcong seemed to get stronger and control more and more of the country.

e a few countries, such as Australia and New Zealand, sent token forces to help the Americans, but most stayed aloof, including Britain. France actually condemned America's action.

4 The end of the war:

a in 1969 the new American President, Richard Nixon, announced that American troops would be gradually withdrawn from Vietnam as the South Vietnamese forces were built up. He was in fact anxious to secure a way out of this costly war.

Peace talks had begun in 1968 in Paris, but achieved nothing until 1973, when a temporary peace was signed between north and south, and the American forces were withdrawn.

b in fact, fighting on a large scale soon broke out again, and without American forces to help them, the South Vietnamese were quickly defeated. Saigon, the South Vietnamese capital, was captured by the Vietcong in April 1975, and the war was over.

Fig. 65 US Marines land to attack Vietcong forces, 1966.

A The 'Roaring Twenties'

1 Introduction:

a during the First World War American industry and farming had expanded rapidly to meet the needs of the Allies for food, weapons and ships, and the USA's own needs when she entered the war on the Allied side in 1917.

b with the end of the war, the USA entered into a spell of 'isolationism'. Congress refused to ratify the Treaty of Versailles or to allow the USA to join the League of Nations.

President Wilson's party, the Democrats, were defeated in the elections of 1920 and a Republican President, W. G. Harding, who had offered a 'return to normalcy' was elected, backed by a Republican Congress.

c the Republicans were the party of 'big business' and believed in as little state interference as possible. During the 1920s their policies seemed to work. The USA entered a spell of industrial prosperity greater than ever before. Business boomed e.g. the number of cars in use more than trebled.

As a result, after Harding's death in 1923 his Republican successor, Calvin Coolidge, had no difficulty in winning the 1924 Presidential election, with the slogan 'Keep cool with Coolidge'. When Coolidge declined to stand in 1928, Herbert Hoover, another Republican, became President.

d yet not all shared in this prosperity. Although industrial output increased by 60% in the 1920s, the working man's real wages only rose by about 10%. (This meant that the rich enjoyed great wealth.) Also, farming was not prosperous. In general, American farmers tended to produce too much, and as a result prices for their crops fell.

e in these years the government interfered to increase tariffs and limit immigration.

The Fordney-McComber (1922) and Smoot-Hartley (1930) tariffs were high. This was to protect American industries from foreign competition. Yet this policy meant that other countries were stopped from exporting to the USA and so could not afford to buy from her. Also, they put up tariff barriers against the USA in return.

Traditionally, the USA had welcomed all immigrants. By the Immigration Act of 1924, however, this policy was ended. The act limited new immigrants from any one country in any one year to 3% of the number born in that country already living in the USA.

f the early twenties were the years of a big 'Red scare' in America. Communist plots were suspected everywhere, and thousands of radicals and Socialists were arrested. Big business used this climate of opinion to crush attempts to form trade unions by working people. Employers did not hesitate to use gangs of thugs to break strikes for better wages and conditions. Police and even troops were called in and used against striking coal miners and steel workers.

g the most infamous example of the Red scare was the case of Sacco and Vanzetti, two radical anarchists who were convicted in 1921, after an unfair trial, of murder in the course of an attempted payroll robbery. Their guilt was very doubtful, and world opinion was strongly in their favour, yet after numerous appeals had been rejected they were executed in 1927.

2 Prohibition. This was a ban on the manufacture, importation and dealing in alcoholic drink, such as beer, wine and spirits, and resulted from the Eighteenth Amendment to the Constitution, which Americans voted for in 1919, and the Volstead Act which gave the government power to enforce it. However, vast numbers of Americans wanted to go on drinking, and this led to widespread evasion and then to gangsterism:

a hoodlums such as Al Capone realised that there was a fortune to be made in evading prohibition, and built up vast 'bootlegging' empires to make, import and sell liquor.

Illicit stills were set up to manufacture drinks such as 'bathtub gin', or industrial alcohol was treated to make it drinkable. Serious illness or even death sometimes resulted from drinking it.

Much 'booze' was imported by ship from abroad, or by road from Canada. Gun battles between rival bootlegging gangs often resulted from attempts to 'hijack' shipments of liquor, or for control of a rival gang's 'territory' in a city.

b too few government agents were appointed to enforce the act, and the local police forces in e.g. Chicago, became riddled with corruption, as officers accepted bribes from gangsters to turn a blind eye to their activities. Thus tens of thousands of 'speakeasies' (illegal drinking places) remained open despite prohibition.

c those who had supported what they called the 'noble experiment' began to realise that they had made a bad mistake. Yet not until 1933 was prohibition ended.

3 The 'Crash' of 1929. During the 1920s prices of shares on the American stock exchanges rose steadily to dizzy heights. It seemed that no investor could lose. As a result Americans of all classes speculated in shares, i.e. bought them to sell again when the price rose, as it always seemed to do.

However, because of the low level of wages, the depressed state of farming and tariff barriers abroad, by late 1929 American industry had reached the point where it could not sell all it manufactured. Thus profits were bound to fall, as were share prices:

a starting in September 1929 share prices started to fall. Panic set in as speculators all began to sell their shares before the prices fell further, while nobody wanted to buy. Thus on 'Black Thursday' (24 October) the biggest ever share price fall in one day was recorded in New York. These events were known as the 'Wall Street Crash' (Wall Street, New York, is the home of the USA's biggest stock exchange).

b in the next two years shares lost two-thirds of their value. Many investors were ruined by the crash and the depression which followed. Foreign trade fell. Factories closed and workers were laid off. Dividends fell, banks collapsed and prices of most goods and farm produce dropped. People could not afford to buy so much, and this led to further decline in business, with more sackings. Soon the number of unemployed reached the staggering figure of fifteen million.

c President Hoover did little, as he believed that prosperity was 'just around the corner'. His government did set up a Reconstruction Finance Corporation to make loans to businesses, but little else.

As a result, the Democratic candidate, Franklin Delano Roosevelt, easily defeated Hoover in the Presidential election of 1932, and the Democrats gained control of Congress.

d during the election campaign, Roosevelt had called for a 'New deal for the American people', and the phrase 'New Deal' was used to describe his programme on taking office.

Fig. 66   President Roosevelt, 1882-1945.

Fig. 67   A typical scene during the prohibition era, aftermath of a gang fight, 1933.

B America under Roosevelt

1 F. D. Roosevelt came from an old and wealthy family. He was stricken with polio in 1921, which cost him much of the use of his legs, and meant he had to use a wheel chair or sticks. Nevertheless, he stood as Democratic candidate for the post of Governor of New York in 1928 and won:

a after becoming President in 1933 (the President takes office early in the year following the Presidential election of the previous November) he was re-elected President three times, in 1936, 1940 and 1944. However, worn out by the strain of war, he died suddenly in April 1945, to be succeeded by his Vice-President, Harry S. Truman.

b 'FDR', as he was called, was the opposite of Hoover. He believed the government could cure the depression, and must act with vigour to do so. Also, he had great confidence in America's strength, a confidence which he put across to the American people in his speeches, especially in his 'fireside chats', talks over the radio. On taking office he said in a famous speech: 'The only thing we have to fear is fear itself'.

2 The 'Hundred Days'. In the first three months of Roosevelt's Presidency, March–June 1933, Congress passed a series of measures designed to put the country on its feet again:

a on taking office, Roosevelt closed all the USA's banks to stop panic withdrawals of deposits. Then, in the space of a few days, Congress passed an Emergency Banking Act, which gave the government powers to help the banks over the crisis.
Roosevelt went on the air and explained to the American people what he had done. As a result confidence was restored, and many re-deposited their money in a bank. In June another Banking Act was passed to stop banks speculating on the stock exchange.

b to help farmers, the Agricultural Adjustment Act (AAA) was passed. This provided for government subsidies to be paid to farmers in return for producing less, and led to better prices for their produce.
An Emergency Farm Mortgage Act and a Farm Credit Act made government loans available, to stop farmers being turned off their lands because they could not pay their mortgages.

c for houseowners, a Home Owners' Loan Corporation (HOLC) and a Federal Housing Administration (FHA) were set up to help with loans towards mortgage repayments.

d the Tennessee Valley Authority (TVA) was set up to construct a series of dams and irrigation projects to provide electricity and adequate water to a backward and poor farming area. Farmers in the region were taught the latest methods of growing better crops and conserving the soil. The scheme was a great success.

e to provide jobs, a Civilian Conservation Corps (CCC) was formed. This employed up to half a million young men to plant forests and create parks and campsites.

f there had been no government money available to help the unemployed or old people. Roosevelt created the Federal Emergency Relief Administration (FERA), with funds of $500,000,000 to provide relief for them.

g a National Recovery Act was not so successful. This aimed to secure the help of industry to limit excess production and wasteful competition. At the same time, hours of work were to be limited, workers were to be allowed to form unions for collective bargaining, and child labour was to be abolished.
However, many businessmen refused to join the scheme, which was voluntary, and the Supreme Court later declared the scheme illegal (as it did to some of Roosevelt's measures to help farmers).

3 Further reforms:

a agriculture continued to benefit from government subsidies and loans. In times of surplus the government bought excess produce and stored it to stop prices falling too much.
In some parts of the USA bad farming methods had led to the creation of 'dust bowls' where the soil was turned into sand by drought. The Soil Conservation Act of 1936 helped to stop this, by encouraging the planting of belts of trees and new grasses.
A Rural Electrical Administration was set up

to bring electricity to country districts.

b on taking office, Roosevelt had taken the USA off the gold standard, and made all payments legal in paper money. He went on to devalue the dollar to make America's exports cheaper. Acts in 1933 and 1934 helped the government to prevent the formation of fraudulent companies.

c though unemployment was not conquered in the USA until the Second World War, working people benefited from many government measures under Roosevelt.

A Works Progress Administration (WPA) was started to provide jobs for the unemployed on projects such as building roads and airports. A National Youth Administration (NYA) provided work for young people.

A National Labour Relations Board (NLRB) was founded in 1935 to help workers secure better conditions through collective bargaining with their employers.

A Fair Labour Standards Act of 1938 established a minimum wage and maximum working hours.

d a milestone was the Social Security Act of 1935. This provided Federal aid for the old, the handicapped and dependent children, and started a scheme of unemployment insurance. The system has since been greatly extended.

e though opposed bitterly by some Americans who were against state control in any disguise, Roosevelt's measures were highly popular with most of the American people, especially industrial workers and farmers. Recovery did not come as quickly as he had hoped it would, however, and in 1939 there were still 4 000 000 unemployed in the USA.

4 The United States in wartime:

a isolationism was strong in the USA until Pearl Harbor. Then America threw herself wholeheartedly into the war effort.

b although 15 000 000 Americans were called up to serve in the armed forces, output from the factories doubled, and huge amounts of guns, aircraft, tanks and ships were produced. Thus the USA became, in Roosevelt's words 'the arsenal of democracy' and supplied the Allies all over the world with the means to fight.

c farming prospered, encouraged by the need to export large amounts of foodstuffs to the Allied nations.

d the USA suffered no material damage from the war, and she emerged from it as the richest and most powerful nation in the world.

Fig. 68   The 'arsenal of democracy'. Mass production of Boeing 'Flying Fortress' bombers, 1944.

C Post-war America

1 The Truman administration. Roosevelt's successor, Harry S. Truman, took office when World War II was nearly over. He went on to win a surprise victory in the Presidential election of 1948, when all the experts had predicted a Republican victory. He refused to contest the election of 1952, which was won by the Republican candidate, Dwight D. Eisenhower:

a Truman wanted to introduce a 'Fair Deal' designed to extend the system of social security, and provide better pensions. However, Congress, which had a Republican majority, rejected the scheme. A Civil Rights Bill suffered the same fate.

b Negroes in the USA suffered from discrimination against them because of their race. They were kept out of many good jobs. Their housing was worse than white peoples'. Their children often had to go to separate and inferior schools. In hotels and restaurants, and on buses, they might have to sit separately from white people. Negroes were often not allowed to vote, much less stand as candidates in elections.

c this discrimination was worst in the southern states, where the Negroes had once been slaves. There, a Negro who protested could be beaten up or lynched, possibly by the Ku Klux Klan, a white terrorist organisation aimed at maintaining white supremacy, and keeping the Negroes 'in their place'. Truman's Civil Rights Bill, to ensure that Negroes could vote freely in elections, was rejected by Congress.

2 The Eisenhower years, 1953–61. Dwight D. Eisenhower was not a Roosevelt type of President. He left the work of government to his Ministers, yet he was widely popular and trusted in the USA and throughout the free world, and easily secured re-election in 1956:

a Eisenhower acted vigorously, however, to secure civil rights for America's Negroes. Earl Warren, appointed Chief Justice of the Supreme Court by Eisenhower, declared that segregation in schools was illegal. When rioting followed an attempt by two Negro children to enrol in an all-white school in the town of Little Rock, Arkansas, Eisenhower sent in troops to ensure the children's admission.

b since then, American Negroes have gradually ended this discrimination, led in peaceful demonstration by leaders such as Martin Luther King (who was, however, assassinated in 1968).

At the same time, many Negroes have drifted from the south to the cities of the north and west, where they often live in squalid ghettoes. This has led many of them, especially the young, to support violent groups such as the Black Panthers and Black Muslims.

c one unsavoury episode in the early 1950s was the rise of Senator Joe McCarthy. He made a name for himself by promoting a Red scare, at a time soon after the fall of China to the Communists, while America was fighting Communism in Korea, and when Russian spies were active in most western countries. Some, such as the Rosenbergs (man and wife) had betrayed vital American secrets about the atomic bomb to their masters. McCarthy, however, saw Red spies everywhere, in America's civil service, the State Department, the White House and the forces.

d in his 'witch-hunt' McCarthy, as leader of the Senate's 'Un-American Activities' investigation committee, mercilessly grilled and browbeat hundreds of innocent people to try to prove that they were Communist sympathisers, some of whom lost friends and jobs as a result. Eventually, partly because people saw for themselves on television how McCarthy's committee worked, public opinion turned against him and he lost his post in 1954, dying three years later.

3 John F. Kennedy. In 1960 the Democratic candidate, John F. Kennedy, narrowly defeated the Republican Richard Nixon in the Presidential election:

a Kennedy promised the American people a 'New Frontier' programme of reforms, an extension of the New Deal. However, his efforts were unsuccessful to provide e.g. government help for medical care for the elderly, and he had achieved little before his assassination at Dallas, Texas, on 22 November 1963.

b one important step he did take was to pledge the USA in March 1961 to put a man on the Moon by 1970. Russia seemed to have a big lead over the USA in space exploration, and Kennedy was determined, for reasons of prestige as well as defence, that America must catch up (see fig. 70).

4 Lyndon B. Johnson. Vice-President Johnson was sworn in as Kennedy's successor, and went on to win the 1964 election in his own right:

a more successful at managing Congress than Kennedy had been, Johnson embarked on a 'Great Society' programme. Medical aid for the elderly was provided out of government funds (Medicare). More help was given to education, and a Civil Rights Act forbade racial discrimination in housing.

b yet the USA was becoming increasingly divided over the question of the Vietnam War, and there were widespread riots at universities to protest against it. Thus Johnson said he would not contest the next Presidential election. In the 1968 election the Republican Richard Nixon emerged as the next President of the USA.

5 Richard Nixon:

a Nixon was successful in ending the Vietnam War, but only by pulling out American forces and thus ensuring a Communist victory.

b he was re-elected in 1972, but soon ran into serious trouble. The Democratic Party headquarters at Watergate, Washington, had been burgled in June 1972 by Nixon supporters. An investigation into this began in early 1973 and led up to Nixon's resignation in August 1974. The investigators had discovered much corruption and tax evasion among Nixon's associates.

c as Vice-President Agnew had resigned before Nixon, the latter was succeeded by Gerald Ford as President. Ford went on to be narrowly defeated by the Democratic candidate, Jimmy Carter, in the election of 1976.

Fig. 69   President John F. Kennedy, 1917-63.

Fig. 70   American Moon landing of Apollo 15, August 1971. In the 1960s the USA caught up with Russia and then overtook her in the 'space race'. In April 1961 the Russian Yuri Gagarin had become the first man to orbit the Earth. The American John Glenn followed him in February 1962. In June 1966 the unmanned US Surveyor I landed on the Moon. The greatest triumph came in July 1969 when Neil Armstrong and Edwin Aldrin became the first men to land on the Moon.

A Russia under Lenin, 1918–24

1 The Great Civil War and foreign intervention, 1917–20:

a in these years Lenin's régime was threatened by foreign forces and by anti-Communist forces inside Russia (some Tsarist, some Liberal or Socialist, together generally known as 'Whites').

b foreign forces had been landed in Russia to protect supply dumps during the war for use against Germany, and helped the Whites. In the north the British held Archangel and Murmansk, in the south the French held Odessa on the Black Sea, while in the Far East the Japanese held Vladivostok. When the war in western Europe ended, Polish armies invaded Russia to push Poland's frontier eastwards. On the Baltic coast German troops and British warships were active in 1919.

c the government or 'Red' forces were attacked by the Whites from several directions. The White General Yudenitch advanced almost to Petrograd in 1919. In the south, in the Ukraine and Caucasus, General Denikin led the White forces. In Siberia, they were commanded by Admiral Kolchak.

d yet Lenin, and Trotsky, who was in charge of the Red Army, showed great ability in defending their régime. New armies were raised and equipped somehow. The authority of officers, and the death penalty for desertion or cowardice, which had been abolished, were restored.

e the Whites helped to ruin their cause by brutal treatment of prisoners and of peasants in the countryside they conquered. Many Russians, even if anti-Communist, supported the Reds to repel foreign invaders.

f also, foreign intervention was half-hearted. Though Churchill in Britain and Marshal Foch in France wanted a full-scale war to crush Communism in Russia, the peoples of these countries had had enough of fighting. The British Government withdrew its forces from Russia, as did the French after their Black Sea Fleet mutinied.

g thus by 1920 the White forces had been driven out and their leaders exiled or shot.

h to secure peace with his neighbours Lenin recognised the independence of Finland, Latvia, Estonia, Lithuania and Poland. This meant big losses of Russian territory compared with her frontiers of 1914. However, White Russia and the Ukraine, lost by the Treaty of Brest-Litovsk in 1918, became part of Russia again.

2 The war against Germany, the Revolutions of 1917 and the Civil War had left Russia exhausted. Industrial and agricultural output were well below their pre-1914 levels, while food and fuel were desperately short. This led up to a mutiny of the Red Navy at Kronstadt, which was only defeated after heavy fighting.

Lenin now realised that he must abandon his policy of 'War Communism' and introduced his 'New Economic Policy' (NEP) instead.

3 On the farms, the food levy (which had meant that all surplus production above a peasant family's own needs must go to the government) was abolished. A grain tax was introduced instead, and the peasants were allowed to keep part of their surplus for sale. They were also allowed to enlarge their holdings of land, and to hire labour. This suited the 'Kulaks' or richer peasants.

In industry and commerce, private businesses on a small scale were allowed once more. This led to the appearance of a class of 'Nepmen' or well-to-do capitalists.

4 Though opposed by many of Lenin's supporters, the NEP was a big success. In 1921-2, despite this, Russia suffered a disastrous drought and famine in which millions died, and the government asked for foreign aid such as supplies of food, clothing and medicines. By the late 1920s farm and factory output was back to the 1914 level.

5 In 1923 a new Constitution was finally approved for Russia, now the Union of Soviet Socialist Republics (USSR):

a local Soviets elected representatives to a provincial congress, which in turn elected delegates to the All-Russian (later All-Union) Congress of Soviets.

b the Congress elected an executive committee, a 'Council of People's Commissars', who were the real power in the state.

c members of the Soviets were elected by various groups of workers. 'Non-working' groups such as the middle classes and the clergy did not have the vote. Voting was open, i.e. there was no secret ballot. All this ensured that the Communist Party, the only one allowed, stayed in control.

d Russia was in fact a 'police state' under a tyranny as strict as that of any of the Tsars. No open opposition to the government was allowed. The churches were persecuted. The press, and later radio and TV, were strictly censored. Political offenders were liable to arrest and torture or 'brainwashing' by the dreaded secret police, and then to imprisonment, perhaps in a labour camp, or execution without trial.

6 The death of Lenin, 1924:

a Lenin had worked very hard and successfully, and led his country through terrible difficulties. (The city of Petrograd was renamed Leningrad in his honour.) On his death in 1924 he expressed grave doubts, in his will, as to the ability of either Stalin (General Secretary of the Communist Party) or Trotsky to succeed him.

b however, his will was kept secret, and so a struggle developed between Stalin and Trotsky for the leadership. The struggle lasted for several years, before Stalin emerged successful in 1927. Trotsky was later banished from Russia, and assassinated on Stalin's orders in Mexico in 1940.

7 There were considerable policy differences between the two. Trotsky wanted to spread the revolution throughout the world at once. Stalin wanted to build up Russia's strength first, advocating a policy of 'Socialism in one country'. Inside Russia, Trotsky wanted to move more rapidly than Stalin in bringing about a Communist system, in such matters as collective farming.

B Russia under Stalin, 1927–53

1 The Five Year Plans. On Trotsky's fall, Stalin embarked on a series of Five Year Plans, in 1928, 1933 and 1938. Agriculture, and all industries, were set high targets of growth and output, which were designed to transform

Fig. 71   Joseph Stalin, 1879-1953.

Russia into a leading industrial nation. The plans marked the end of the NEP:

a industrially, the stress was on heavy industry, i.e. plants for making iron and steel, coal mines, power stations and machinery for use in factories. Consumer goods, such as cars, bicycles and even the necessities of life such as housing and clothing, had to wait.

b a vast electrification programme was carried out e.g. the building of a huge dam at Dnepropetrovsk to produce hydro-electric power.

c railways and canals were built, for instance the Moscow-Volga Canal, and huge industrial towns grew up, such as Magnitogorsk and Stalingrad.

d labour was virtually conscripted to work on the new projects under primitive conditions for low wages, yet the plans mostly succeeded. By 1939 Russia was producing five or six times as much coal, iron and steel as in 1913.

e on the land, Stalin's plans for collective farms, which meant that the peasants had to pool their land and farm it under government control, met widespread opposition. In some areas, e.g. the Ukraine, there was virtual civil war. The rich peasants or Kulaks murdered Communist officials, and the army had to be called in. Even then the Kulaks burnt their buildings and crops, and slaughtered their cattle, rather than hand them over. Thousands of people were killed, and farm output fell below the 1913 level, resulting in another famine in the early 1930s.

f Stalin was forced to slow the pace of collectivisation, and the peasants were allowed to retain plots of land for their own use, and to sell what they produced on them. Thanks to this compromise, and much investment of government money in farm machinery, e.g. tractors, production rose again.

2 The purges of the 1930s. The years leading up to the Second World War saw a remarkable series of purges and treason trials in Russia which have never been fully explained:

a hundreds of thousands of people were put to death after sham trials. One thing which puzzled many in the west was the fact that those who were brought to trial in open court always pleaded guilty to all charges brought against them.

b in the early 1930s, many technicians and industrial managers, including British engineers working on contracts in Russia, were found guilty of 'sabotage' (though the Britons were allowed to leave Russia).

c then in December 1934 the assassination of Stalin's right-hand man, Serge Kirov, the Governor of Leningrad, sparked off a series of purges and trials which lasted until 1938. By the time these were over, Stalin's old Bolshevik colleagues, such as Zinoviev and Kamenev, had been executed along with many others for 'treason' or 'Trotskyist plots', as had tens of thousands of army officers and most of Russia's generals. (This led many in the west to believe that the Red Army had been seriously weakened, and would be of little use in a war with Germany.)

d millions more were sent to labour camps or prison. Towards the end of the purges, the chief of Stalin's secret police (the NKVD) and many of his men, who had carried out Stalin's death sentences, suffered the same fate themselves.

3 The Constitution of 1936. Despite the purges, Stalin found time to introduce a new Constitution for Russia:

a Russia was to have eleven member Republics. The new Parliament for the USSR was to be called the Supreme Soviet. It was of two houses, the Council of the Union, representing the people of the USSR as a whole (elected by all over 18), and the Council of Nationalities. The Supreme Soviet chose the Praesidium to act for it when not in session, and the Council of People's Commissars, the equivalent of the British Cabinet.

b this Constitution made no difference to the fact that the Communist Party rules Russia. The Supreme Soviet meets, usually, twice a year for a fortnight, and there are no debates. The members listen to what their leaders have to say and then vote. In the elections, only Communist candidates can stand, and although voting is supposed to be secret, it is possible to tell if an elector has cast a vote against the party's candidate.

4 Stalin in wartime, 1939–45:

a during the war with Germany (The Great Patriotic war) Russia suffered terribly. Millions were killed in battle and millions more died under German rule in occupied Russia. Yet Russia adopted a 'scorched earth' policy. To stop Germany from reaping the fruits of her early victories, factories, bridges, railways, oil wells, dams, farms, and crops were destroyed rather than be allowed to fall into German hands.

b many factories were evacuated eastwards beyond the Ural Mountains, and huge new industrial centres were developed to produce guns, tanks and aircraft to defeat Germany.

c all Russia rallied to Stalin's leadership. Though he seems to have lost his nerve for a few days after being taken by surprise by the German attack, he recovered and proved a tough war leader. He even appealed for, and received, the blessing of the churches, which had been persecuted severely under his rule.

5 Recovery postwar, 1945–53:

a helped partly by the plundering of German factories and raw materials at the end of the war, Russian industry and agriculture recovered well from the effects of war. In the factories, the emphasis was still on heavy industry, and on production of war material during the 'Cold War'.

b the years before Stalin's death saw a growth of a Stalin 'personality cult', rather akin to the worship of Hitler and Mussolini in their countries in their heyday. Pictures and statues of Stalin were everywhere. Towns, factories and streets were named after him. His name and achievements were always being mentioned in the press and on the radio.

c he developed the 'party line' to cover all aspects of life. For instance, poets whose work was considered 'bourgeois' (middle class) were forced to recant, as were authors of suspect fiction. Composers of music were made to do the same.

Even in science, Stalin's favourite, the biologist Lysenko, laid down theories of genetics that were in accordance with the party's thinking, and different from those taught in the west.

C Russia since Stalin

Stalin's death on 5 March 1953 marked the end of an era for Russia.

1 His successors were to change his policies in many ways:

a in foreign affairs the 'Cold War' was replaced by the 'Thaw' and policies of peaceful co-existence with the west.

b in domestic policies, 'de-Stalinisation' meant more individual freedom (though still not much by western standards), less power for the secret police (whose chief from Stalin's time, Beria, was executed), and the possibility of voicing limited criticism of the régime. Political offenders were now more likely to be sent to a mental hospital to silence their criticism, rather than to be shot.

c industrially, more consumer goods were produced, and less was spent on heavy industry and armaments.

2 His immediate successors were Malenkov and Nikita Khrushchev. The latter became Russia's leader in 1956. In a very important speech to the twentieth Conference of the Soviet Communist Party in February 1956, Khrushchev attacked many features of Stalin's rule. In particular, he denounced Stalin's personality cult, the purges and treason trials of the 1930s and Stalin's failure to prepare for the war with Germany adequately.

3 Russia scored great triumphs in space exploration in the late 1950s and the 1960s. In October 1957 she sent the first man-made Earth satellite, Sputnik I, into orbit; and in April 1961 Major Yuri Gagarin became the first man to orbit the Earth in space.

Yet this space programme cost vast amounts of money. Khrushchev tried to prune expenditure by cuts in 'conventional' forces, and by greater reliance on rockets and atomic weapons.

4 In agriculture, production failed to reach the target set, and in 1963 a bad harvest forced Russia to the humiliation of buying grain from the USA, as she has continued to do.

5 In 1964 Khrushchev lost his position as leader. His opponents taxed him with many failings, but it would seem that his risky foreign policy and his failings in agriculture were his undoing. He was replaced by two men, Leonid Brezhnev and Alexei Kosygin.

These two announced measures designed to increase industrial output by giving managers more freedom of decision and less government control, with some profit sharing as an incentive. In agriculture, steps to increase production failed, partly because of bad weather, which forced Russia to buy more grain from the USA.

Fig. 72 Yuri Gagarin, 1934-68.

A Introduction

The thirty years after the ending of the Second World War in 1945 saw great changes in Britain and her position in the world.

1 At home, the 'Welfare State' was established, mass unemployment was conquered, and there was a big rise in the standard of living of the British people as a whole.

2 Abroad, Britain lost her position as a world power, mainly because the power and economic strength of the USA and Russia far outstripped hers.

3 Also, the Empire broke up. By 1975 most of it had asked for, and been given, independence, and ties with Britain as the 'mother country' were usually weak.

B Britain's position in 1945

1 Immediate problems:

    a there was a serious housing shortage, as almost one-fifth of Britain's homes had been destroyed or damaged by German bombing, and no new houses had been built for the six years of the war.

    b many of Britain's industries, such as the railways and coal mining, had been worked flat-out during the war with little time for vital maintenance work. They were in poor shape.

    c there were millions of men and women to be demobilised from the forces. This was done quite smoothly.

2 Long-term problems. Post-war Britain faced two problems which have baffled successive governments in the years since 1945:

    a one is inflation. This means rising prices and wages. One cause has been full employment, which has made it easy for workers to press wage demands. Rising wages have usually meant rising prices, as firms have had to increase their prices to pay their workers more. Prices have risen too, at times, because Britain imports much of her food and raw materials, e.g. wheat and oil, and has to pay more for them if world prices rise.

    b inflation is a serious matter because people living on a fixed income, e.g. pensioners, find themselves worse off as prices rise. Inflation cuts the value of the pound, and puts up the price of British exports, so that other countries may buy elsewhere instead.

    c the 'balance of payments' is the second serious problem. If Britain buys more from foreign countries than they do from her, she faces a 'trade gap'.

Before 1939 Britain had large 'invisible earnings' from insurance and banking services to the rest of the world, and from interest on her investments abroad, as well as earnings by British shipping. These earnings were enough to cover her trade gap, and give her a favourable balance of payments, i.e. other countries paid Britain more than she paid them.

    d during the Second World War, however, Britain had to sell many investments abroad, and lost a lot of shipping trade. This meant that after 1945, to reach a favourable balance of payments, Britain had to export more, or import less, or both, than in 1939. In some years she has failed badly.

Fig. 73 Strike scene, 1956. Since 1945 strikes have sometimes caused serious hold-ups, as in the car industry. Yet Britain has suffered less from strikes than many other countries.

C The Labour Government of 1945–51

This government did much to improve the social well-being of the British people, but was faced with very difficult economic problems which it only partly solved.

1 The immediate need for foreign trade was a quick growth in exports. To pay for the raw materials for these Britain needed American dollars. Unfortunately she had sold most investments in the USA. Therefore a dollar loan was needed at once. J. M. Keynes, the famous economist, was sent to the USA in 1945 to negotiate this. He succeeded. America lent Britain $3,750 million, to be repaid over fifty years at 2% interest.

2 The British Government continued rationing and controls, such as those on raw materials. Sir Stafford Cripps, as Chancellor of the Exchequer, introduced a policy of 'austerity', meaning that Britain had to consume less to help the balance of payments, by exporting more and importing less.

3 Exports were badly hit by a fuel crisis during the severe winter of 1946–7. Coal stocks were low, and heavy blizzards hampered transport, causing some power stations and many factories to close.

4 in 1948–9 exports fell and the British Government was forced to devalue the pound. It was now valued at $2.80, instead of $4.03. This meant that British goods were cheaper for foreigners to buy, so exports increased. However, all the things she imported, such as food and raw materials, would cost more. Thus devaluation was not a permanent solution to Britain's problems.

5 in June 1950 the Korean War broke out, and caused world prices of raw materials to soar. This led to a fast rise in prices in Britain, and a bad balance of payments deficit.

This contributed to the Labour Government's defeat by the Conservatives, led by Churchill, in the general election of 1951.

6 Yet the Labour Government had achieved much. There were jobs for all. Wages had risen. It had shown that unemployment could be beaten in peacetime.

7 It nationalised several important industries and the Bank of England:

a the coal mines in 1946.
b electricity generation and supply in 1947.
c railways, canals and road haulage in 1947.
d the gas industry in 1948.
e iron and steel in 1949.
f the Cable and Wireless Company in 1949.

8 The Representation of the People Act, 1948, abolished the business franchise. This had meant that owners of business premises, e.g. a shop or office, had a second vote.

In 1949 the delaying power of the House of Lords' veto was reduced from two years to one.

9 In general, the Labour Party favoured building council houses for rent, while the Conservatives favoured building private houses for sale. In 1945–51, one and a quarter million houses were built, a good achievement considering the many shortages of those years, but not enough to solve the problem.

Fig. 74 A factory in a 'development area' near Glasgow. In such areas the government encourages firms to build factories to provide jobs.

D The 'Welfare State'

The Welfare State had its origins in the Beveridge Report, 1942. Early in the Second World War the government began to make plans for new social services. Sir William (later Lord) Beveridge, was Chairman of the committee set up to consider these. Its report said:

1 Poverty was caused by loss of earnings by the family breadwinner, as a result of illness or unemployment, especially among large families.

2 A plan for 'social security' was suggested. This was defined as 'Security for the individual organised by the State' in case of sickness, unemployment or old age. This would be achieved by a 'welfare state' which would abolish 'want, disease, squalor, ignorance and illness'.

3 To do this, an insurance scheme, compulsory for all, would guarantee a minimum income in times of sickness, unemployment and when a person became too old to work. The scheme would also pay for a National Health Service to provide free medical treatment for all, and would enable the state to pay family allowances to those with children.

This last was actually the first part of the scheme to come into force. The Children's Allowances Act of 1945, passed under Churchill's Coalition Government, provided for weekly allowances for all children except the first.

Fig. 75 Aneurin Bevan (1897-1960), founder of the National Health Service.

4 Under the Premiership of Clement Attlee, the Labour Government of 1945–51 put the rest of the Beveridge Plan into force.

5 The National Insurance Act of 1946 set up the present system:

a National Insurance, started in 1911 by Lloyd George, was now extended to cover all working adults.

b employers, too, had to pay. For many years this was done by means of stamps on their employees' insurance cards.

c in return, the insured person is paid a weekly benefit when unemployed or ill.

d men (at 65) and women (at 60) become eligible for the Old Age Pension.

e other benefits include maternity grants (payable on the birth of a child), death grants to help cover funeral expenses, and widows' pensions.

6 The National Health Service Act, 1946, set up a free comprehensive medical service for all, providing free medical, dental, optical, and hospital treatment:

a most of Britain's hospitals were to be taken over by the state and run by fourteen Regional Hospital Boards.

b the act provided for maternity care, health visiting and child welfare clinics, run by local authorities.

c doctors, opticians and dentists were to be paid by the government.

d the act was the work of the fiery Aneurin Bevan, Minister of Health, who nevertheless displayed great tact and skill in persuading the British Medical Association to agree to join the scheme. Doctors and dentists, etc. had feared a loss of independence, prestige and earnings if they entered the scheme.

7 The National Insurance (Industrial Injuries) Act 1946, provided special benefits and even disablement pensions for people injured at work.

8 The National Assistance Act 1948, set up a National Assistance Board which replaced the old Public Assistance Committees:

a it would provide additional benefits for all people whose income was below a certain level e.g. a pensioner who might have to pay a high rent.

b it was intended that few would need to

apply for National Assistance (now called Supplementary Benefit), but inflation since the war has forced many to do so.

E Conservative Rule, 1951–64

1 When the Conservatives came back to power under Winston Churchill in 1951, there was no large-scale reversal of Labour policies. The new government had no intention of dismantling the Welfare State. In other fields, only iron and steel and road transport were denationalised. However, what remained of rationing was abolished, and many controls on trade and industry were removed.

2 In the years 1951–64 the standard of living for most Britons rose considerably (though not as fast as on the Continent). Harold Macmillan was a successful Minister of Housing, and stepped up the building rate to over 300 000 houses a year. The term 'affluent society' came into use. Production, wages, and exports rose, but so did prices, though more slowly.

3 However, the Conservatives failed to solve the problems of inflation and the balance of payments.

4 Several times the government tried to check inflation (when it was said that the economy was 'over-heating') by:

  a putting up the bank rate. This made borrowing cost more, and so tended to make people spend less.

  b restrictions on hire-purchase e.g. insisting on a certain deposit on an article. This too cut down spending.

These two measures we call a 'credit squeeze'.

  c appeals for wage restraint.

Such steps were called a policy of 'stop-go' by the government's opponents, who said that the Conservatives were encouraging industry to expand one minute, and slow down the next.

F Personalities and Parliament

1 On Churchill's resignation from office in 1954, Anthony Eden, later Lord Avon, became Premier, and under him the Conservatives won the general election of 1955. However, Eden resigned in 1957, following the Suez fiasco.

2 He was succeeded by Macmillan, who proved a brilliant party leader:

  a he took the Conservatives to yet another victory in the general election of 1959, with an increased majority. He coined the phrase 'You never had it so good' to describe the country's prosperity.

  b in 1958 his government introduced life peerages. Before, a peerage, entitling its holder to sit in the House of Lords, had always been hereditary. The life peerages were to be for both sexes, and so women gained the right to sit in the House of Lords.

Fig. 76 Harold Macmillan (b. 1894) in 1963, shortly before his resignation as Prime Minister.

Fig. 77 Harold Wilson (b. 1916) as Prime Minister.

c in 1963 'Supermac' or 'Macwonder', as he was known, resigned through ill-health. He was succeeded by the Foreign Secretary, Lord Home, who stepped down from the House of Lords to become Sir Alec Douglas-Home in the House of Commons.

3 Though a kindly and likeable man, Sir Alec lacked Macmillan's flair, and was held by some to have too much of a 'grouse moor image' to be an electoral success. He proved unable to arrest the decline in his party's fortunes that had set in about 1961.

When he took office, the country's trade figures were poor, productivity in industry was failing to rise quickly enough, and there had been several spy scandals which led some to doubt the government's ability to protect the security of the country.

4 Meanwhile, Hugh Gaitskell, Attlee's successor as Labour Party leader, died in 1963, and was succeeded by Harold Wilson.

5 The latter led Labour to a narrow election victory in 1964, when the Conservative Government's term of office came to an end. Sir Alec Douglas-Home, who had led his party well in the election campaign, stepped down as Conservative Party leader, and was succeeded by Edward Heath.

Labour won another victory in the 1966 general election, increasing their majority in the Commons.

6 Labour made solving the balance of payments problem their main aim, and succeeded, but at high cost:

a taxes were increased, to cut down on spending in Britain.

b a Prices and Incomes Board was set up in 1965, to help cut down rises in both, but had mixed success. A prices and wages 'freeze' had to be introduced.

c despite these measures, the pound was devalued again in November 1967 to $2.40. Inflation continued, and Heath led his party to victory over Labour in the 1970 general election.

7 Edward Heath took office as Prime Minister amid the high hopes of his party. These hopes were not to be realised. A man of vision and great ability, Heath somehow lacked Macmillan's ability to win people over. Heath and his Chancellor of the Exchequer, Anthony Barber (later Lord Barber), could find no solution to the country's economic problems that was widely acceptable.

Faced with a miners' strike over pay in early 1974, Heath called a general election to secure a clear expression of public support for his government.

8 However, Labour won a majority over the Conservatives in the Commons, though not an overall one, and Wilson replaced Heath as Premier. In a further general election in October of the same year, Labour secured a narrow overall majority.

9 By the mid-seventies discoveries of huge deposits of oil under the North Sea gave good cause for believing that by 1980 Britain would be self-sufficient in this vital raw material, and would even be able to export large amounts of it, thus easing considerably the balance of payments difficulties.

G The Common Market

In the mid-1950s steps were taken in Europe which led to the signing of the Treaty of Rome in 1957:

1 Six European countries—France, Western Germany, Italy, Belgium, Holland and Luxembourg joined together to form the European Economic Community (EEC). They agreed to abolish tariffs among themselves and thus set up a 'common market' for member countries, with a joint tariff against outside countries.

2 British membership:

a in 1958 Britain had applied for associate membership, but was turned down.

b in 1963 and again in 1967 approaches by first the Conservative and then the Labour Government for membership were turned down, through the opposition of the French President, General de Gaulle.

c however, in 1972 renewed negotiations succeeded, and Britain joined the Common Market on 1 April 1973. There was still much opposition in Britain to joining and to the terms of entry agreed to, but most people were indifferent.

H The Commonwealth

1 India became independent in 1947, splitting into the two states of India (mostly Hindu) and Pakistan (mostly Moslem). Gandhi was assassinated in the following year. Relations between India and Pakistan were usually bad, and full-scale war broke out between them for a while in 1965. Later, East Pakistan proclaimed its independence as Bangladesh.

2 The other British possessions in the Far East, Burma, Ceylon (now Sri Lanka), Malaya and North Borneo, have all become independent, with only Hong Kong remaining a British colony.

3 In Africa, the 'wind of change' as Harold Macmillan called it, began to blow strongly in the 1950s. Starting with the Gold Coast (now Ghana) under Kwame Nkrumah in 1957, almost the whole of British Africa was given independence usually with Dominion status within the Commonwealth.

The exception was Rhodesia, where the government of Ian Smith, bent on maintaining white supremacy there, declared its independence in November 1965. This Britain and the rest of the world refused to recognise, and in 1976 Smith himself announced that his government would make way for black majority rule.

4 In South Africa, successive Nationalist governments followed a policy of 'Apartheid'. The Nationalists are white, Afrikaans-speaking descendants of the Boers. To them, Apartheid means separate development for blacks and whites. Their opponents say it means racial discrimination and oppression of the blacks in South Africa.

This led to growing friction with the other Commonwealth member states, and caused South Africa to resign from the Commonwealth in May 1961 and become a Republic.

5 In the Caribbean, after the failure of a West Indian Federation set up in 1958, most of the former British possessions, such as Jamaica and Guyana, have gained independence.

I Ulster

1 In the 1960s there was growing pressure from the Catholic 'civil rights' movement in Ulster, who protested that Catholics there were denied equality with Protestants in such matters as housing and jobs. Traditional ill-feeling between Catholics and Protestants (see Ch. 2) was thus revived, and riots broke out in Londonderry in 1966.

2 In the following ten years the situation grew steadily worse. Riots, arson, bombings, murder and assassination became commonplace, carried out by various organisations on both sides.

3 British troops were sent to keep order in 1969, and the Ulster Government at Stormont was abolished in 1972, direct rule from London taking its place. Yet by the mid-1970s no end was in sight for Ulster's troubles.

Fig. 78 British troops man a barricade in Londonderry, Northern Ireland, 1972.